CHAINBREAKERS

CHAIN BREAKERS

A TRUE STORY OF HEALING FROM ABUSE

As told to
Michele R.
Sorensen

Deseret Book Company
Salt Lake City, Utah

Library of Congress Cataloging-in-Publication Data.

Sorensen, Michele R., 1962–
    Chainbreakers : a true story of healing from abuse / as told to
  Michele R. Sorensen.
      p. cm.
    Includes bibliographical references.
    ISBN 0-87579-744-X
    1. Child molesting—Religious aspects—Church of Jesus Christ of
Latter-day Saints. 2. Child molesting—Arizona—Case studies.
3. Adult child sexual abuse victims—Pastoral counseling of—Case
studies. 4. Family—Religious life. 5. Church of Jesus Christ of
Latter-day Saints—Membership. 6. Mormon Church—Membership.
I. Title.
BX8643.C55S67   1993
261.8'32—dc20   93-21678
                                                                           CIP

Printed in the United States of America
10 9 8 7 6 5 4 3 2

Special thanks to John C. Carmen II, M.D.

The experiences recorded here are true. Names and identifying details have been changed, however, to protect family members who are in varying stages of recovery.

Because the Savior's promise of healing transcends all individual circumstances, we share this testimony with hope to heal.

Taking Hold, Letting Go

/ / / / /

in the past, i shut myself in.
i never meant to, but it was
easier that way.
and once the door was closed
i thought i could forget.

/ / /

today i passed a window and
stopped to question what i saw.
could i, from this tattered scape,
find even a trace of beauty?

/ / /

a shred of color weaves its way
through murky past and future view
and my wounded heart smiles—
i turn and find my door.

/ / /

hesitation
in my weakness binds me;
One Voice alone to free the way:
I am with you.

/ / /

with trembling hand on latch
i throw His Strength against the
rust of years . . . to hear, at last,
resistance groan
at rending chains.

/ / /

yesterday i shut myself in.
Today I raised a Latch . . .
and found in my own Self
a Sunrise.

by Jennie W. Bowen
(Used by permission)

/ / / 1 / / /

love the hymns so much that when our bishop called me to teach the Spiritual Living lessons in Relief Society, I asked if I could continue being the chorister, too. Singing the hymns inspires me. I love the spirit they bring into our lives. But sometimes, when I'm teaching a particularly sensitive lesson or leading a tender song, I look into the upturned faces of my sisters and see a pair of sorrowing eyes in which hope has been lost, trust has been torn.

In those moments, my own memories rush to the surface in a wave of compassion. I sing harder, more fervently. Or, if I'm teaching a lesson, I bring it straight back to the core of the gospel: our Redeemer, His love and His sacrifice for us. Even the small seeds planted by a single hymn or a humble testimony can be critically important when a person's trust has been violated.

Some of those women may have kicked, raged, and rebelled against the Savior and His gospel. They may still be fighting against the pricks or stumbling around in a fog of confusion and fear, but I know that He will never stop whispering to them. He keeps calling to them, as He has always been calling to them, in a voice of love—sometimes the only voice of love—from a time they don't want to remember.

But yesterday I wasn't in the Relief Society room to lead the singing or teach a lesson. I had attended a stake meeting there, and I was waiting for my husband to pick me up for a date. Everyone else had left quickly, and I thought I was alone, until I gathered my things and stepped into the hall. Farther down the corridor, a friend of mine was leaning against a doorjamb, as unaware of my presence as I'd been of his. He was looking back into the office where—he's the bishop of a neighboring ward—I supposed he'd recently concluded an interview. His hand was on the doorknob; a set of keys swung in the lock.

"Hello, Dr. Lorenz," I said, my voice breaking the hush of the empty hall. Besides being a bishop, Ben was also our family physician and friend. "I've never seen you alone before, much less standing still."

He looked up suddenly, a comfortable grin spreading across his face. "Elizabeth! Hello! I didn't see you." He pulled the door shut firmly as he spoke, retrieving the jingling keys from the lock, and then turned to shake my hand. "How are you?"

"Fine," I answered. "Fine. But a moment ago, you looked like you were carrying a weighty load."

"Oh, that." He smiled again. "Just wishing and thinking—not a luxury I indulge in very often." It seemed he intended to change the subject quickly, but then he fell silent.

When you've known someone a long time, you can do that. You can opt not to interrupt your thoughts for their arrival . . . just share them. After a moment, Ben looked at me again. I thought he was going to ask after my husband or one of my children, but instead he sighed.

"Someone ill?" I prompted, suddenly realizing how dumb my question sounded. If you're a physician, you're always seeing someone who's sick.

But he didn't laugh. "Not just some*one*. The problem is that there are so many."

I was about to comment on the flu that seemed to have hit every family I knew, when he went on.

"There are so many," he repeated, "and I can't just give them an antibiotic and put them to bed. No pills can take the pain and hurt away."

He took a deep breath and smiled at me. "How come I've

known you all these years and only this week I hear that you're a journalist?"

"Well, I'm not really. I'm a mother right now."

"Majored in journalism?"

"No. I never went to college, but I did work in that field for a while."

"Ever published?" he asked.

"Newspaper want ads," I laughed. "Nothing like a book. How about you?"

"No." He spoke slowly. "I've never written a book, but I've been wanting to for years."

"Me too," I answered, surprised at my own openness. Quickly I asked, "What would you write about?"

Now, Ben Lorenz is my boys' idea of an "awesome cowboy." He has a neatly trimmed beard and wears flannel shirts and big belt buckles with fancy beaded designs or shiny stones and intricate metalwork. Some of those first impressions must have rubbed off on me, too, because I expected he'd write some sort of gun-slinging western.

"I'd write a book on abuse," he said, looking right at me. "Something like a survival book for those who were molested as children."

"Really?" I said, almost jumping out of my shoes.

"Yes." His face was serious. Until that moment, I had thought him an easygoing, unexcitable man. I'd never seen him so somber, so deeply concerned.

"One in four of all the women I treat has been abused. Yet most of them feel so isolated. This isn't something people usually talk about freely."

Boy, you're not kidding! I thought.

"They don't compare notes and say, 'Hey! We have incest in common.' "

It was all I could do to smile at him, though there were hundreds—thousands—of things I could have said.

"I suppose the cause of their loneliness goes back a long way," he continued. "When safety and love are denied to a child by the persons most responsible to provide them, the child's ability to trust is stunted or even lost. That's when the first feelings of being alone begin."

"You're right," I answered, surprising myself again, for I rarely talked openly about a time that ran so deep and dark within me. "Children are remarkable. They understand lots of things without being able to put them into words. They can sense good and evil whenever they really want to."

Ben was looking at me, not too closely but intently. I thought, *What a good feeling it is to be listened to—really listened to.*

"Children give their trust so freely," I heard myself say. "They want to give their devotion to the person who is their caregiver. They want more than anything to be safe in that person's love." I paused to see if Ben was still listening. He was. "Then, when their trust is betrayed . . . well, it's like chaos and confusion exploding on their world. That betrayal twists and distorts their vision of everything."

"They become afraid to trust," he said softly.

"They become afraid to trust."

The church building was now entirely empty except for us. Outside the winter air was bitter cold, but the hallway where we stood was warm and well lit, uncluttered and orderly. Ben was thoughtful, listening to what I'd said and thinking. My mind was as calm as our surroundings, yet it hurtled back over years with intense clarity. Recollections focused in my thoughts with such power that not only could I see the incidents of my life but I could feel and smell and taste them as well.

The memories swept backward to the first time I met the man who was to be my "protector." Somehow I knew that all the things a father is supposed to be were missing from his character, yet I was told to call him Daddy.

/ / / / /

My baby sister, Maria, and I came shuffling out of our bedroom. Our too-big slippers made a fun, flopping sound as we walked across the kitchen linoleum through the front room to the bathroom door. My flowered jammies felt soft and warm as the last rich rays of the sun.

Tonight we were going to sleep over at Nanny Julie's house. And we'd gotten ready all by ourselves, just as Mama had asked. I had my favorite stuffed bunny, and Maria had her fuzzy blankie. Together we peeked around the corner into the bathroom.

Mama was looking in the mirror and singing. She was so pretty! Her long auburn hair reached past her waist, and her eyes were a deep, sparkly green, like a piece of wet Navajo jade. Nowadays I would describe her as very petite—almost five feet tall and not quite ninety pounds—but if anyone had asked me to describe her back then, I would have said she was like the china dolls I'd seen in the windows of fancy stores.

"She's doing that beauty school thing again," I whispered to Maria. "Mommy's going to a date."

Maria stifled a giggle—she giggled at everything.

I knew how to read the little hand on the clock, and Mama had been in the bathroom for at least two hours. She'd taken her morning bath again in the evening, styled and restyled her hair, painted her face, changed her clothes three times, and finally chosen jewelry that would do. She looked in the mirror and turned from side to side, examining every inch of her appearance and criticizing it colorfully under her breath. Finally she turned around and looked at us. "Well?"

Our grins could have burst our faces as we cheered. "You're bootiful," Maria beamed.

"You sure?" Mommy asked, turning to me.

"Oh, yes," I said. "Oh, yes! Oh, yes!"

Someone knocked loudly at the door, and Mommy jumped. Maria and I went to answer it, while she did the proper thing by waiting in her room so as not to look anxious. Mama had told me exactly what to do and say, but before I let him in, I pulled the door open a bit and peeked through the crack.

The man looked just as Mommy had described him over the telephone to Nanny Julie. He was tall and slender but not skinny. His light brown hair was cut so short I thought maybe he was bald under his baseball cap. Disrespectfully, I wondered if his big ears were holding the cap in place. But I didn't wonder long, because he was staring down at me with impatient gray eyes.

Mommy was right. He wasn't ugly, but he wasn't handsome. He sure didn't look anything like the little picture she kept on her nightstand. That man had gentle dark eyes and wavy black hair, and Mommy always called him her first love.

I pulled back on the knob, and the door creaked wide open.

The man seemed surprised that someone taller hadn't opened it. But rather than bend over, he looked down his nose and through the screen door at me.

"Hello. How do you do, sir?" I recited just as I had been instructed. "Would you please come in?"

He swung the screen door open abruptly and took a large step into the house. When I offered him a chair, he said he didn't want to sit down. He spread his feet apart and stood by the door, his arms crossed over his chest.

Maria and I ran for our mother's bedroom. "He's here!" she chirped. "He's here!"

"And he's wearing perfume, too!" I added, feeling very important.

Swinging her hair back over her shoulder, Mommy took a deep breath. Then, holding each of us by the hand, she walked out into the front room.

For the next several weeks, these events were repeated over and over until they became almost routine. Even though the man (Mommy called him Chuck) never spoke to Maria and me, we talked a lot about him between ourselves. I couldn't have explained why, but there was one thing I knew for sure: I didn't like him. Maria didn't like him, either, so surely Mama couldn't. He would quit coming soon. Besides, she had other friends. She was pretty, and all the guys at the grocery store thought so, too.

But Chuck kept coming over more and more often. Soon he was hanging around our house a lot, and it was making Mama nervous.

We had a little secret at our house, and Mommy didn't want him to find out about it. She tried hard to keep Chuck in the front room. She always changed the radio to his favorite station whenever he came in. She brought him ice water right away and kept a bowl of extra ice in the freezer just for him. She made sure he never had to get up for anything.

But one afternoon she goofed and excused herself to go to the bathroom. Maria and I were playing together in our room, so no one was around when Chuck ran out of ice water. Our bedroom was at the opposite end of the hall from the kitchen, so we both looked up when we suddenly heard his footsteps on the linoleum. He helped himself to a second glass of water. We watched silently as he opened both doors on the fridge. Looking in there was a no-no. That was Mommy's fridge. Then Chuck looked into the kitchen cupboards, shutting each door soundlessly before he went back into the front room.

I grabbed Maria's arm and pulled her into the corner of our bedroom. "Chuck's in big trouble now!" I gloated. "He knows Mommy's secret." Then, lowering my voice to match the seriousness of his mistake, I added, "And she ain't gonna like that one bit!"

Chuck didn't stay much longer that night, and as soon as he was gone, Maria and I tattled on him. But to our surprise, Mommy got cross. She sent *us* to bed!

The next morning there was a lot of loud knocking at our front door before even Mommy was awake. As she threw on her bathrobe, we fell in right behind her, still half-asleep but curious.

Chuck was the one making all the noise. "Good morning!" he hollered and marched right in the door as soon as Mommy unlocked it. He had two big sacks, one under each arm, that he carried straight into the kitchen and dropped on the counter. He turned around quickly and looked at the three of us. He laughed. In and out of the house Chuck hurried, carrying more and more sacks. Maria and I sat down out of the way and watched. Mommy was standing awfully still, staring at him with her green eyes very big and her mouth sort of twitchy. Then all at once she began to bawl.

Chuck stopped in his tracks.

"You shouldn't have," she cried. "You shouldn't have!"

Chuck put his arms around my mother.

"You shouldn't have, Chuck." She was sobbing even harder now.

I jumped up and screamed, "Don't touch my mommy!" Frantically I started pushing at Chuck's knees. "Go away!"

Chuck looked down at me. His eyes were hard and very angry. I thought he was going to kick me, but I didn't care. "Go 'way!" I yelled again.

Then Mommy got angry, too. She sent me to my room. Maria followed, and we sat together on the floor. We could still see them in the kitchen, though. Chuck kept his arms around our mother until she stopped crying. Then they unloaded those big brown sacks together. It took a long time, but the fridge and cupboards were all full when they finished.

After that, they fixed a huge breakfast of flapjacks and maple syrup, orange juice and pork links. When it was ready, they called us in. Maria and I could eat on TV trays in our bedroom; Mommy and Chuck were going to eat alone at the table. And eat we did! Maria said maybe she was going to pop, and I *knew* I was. We were so busy eating we forgot to listen to what was going on in the kitchen.

But even after the breakfast dishes were all washed, Chuck and our mother kept talking for hours. Maria and I played in our room as we were told, but we knew something strange was happening. We'd never heard Mommy talk this much to any-one before.

I didn't like what was going on. Chuck had really done it now. Mama seemed to think he was wonderful, and that made me shudder. Something inside told me he was a bad man, and I wondered why Mommy didn't know it.

Nothing was the same for the next couple of weeks after Chuck and the groceries arrived. He practically lived at our house. But then one morning everything was different. Chuck wasn't there, and Mommy was absolutely buzzing through all the rooms, washing clothes and packing her pretty yellow travel bag. She also put clothes and toothbrushes for us in a paper sack. Then she sat us down and talked to us about our manners.

We would be needing them because we were going on a sleepover at Nanny Julie's. We would be staying two whole days.

Maria looped her chubby arms around Mama's neck. "Where goin'?"

"Nevada," Mommy said with a smile.

"What for?" I asked, convinced that Mommy realized how four-year-olds understand these things better than three-year-olds do.

"Because," she said, getting up.

I hated that answer. It was the one she used every time she wasn't paying attention or was keeping an adult secret. Then Mommy did the strangest thing of all. She walked over to the nightstand and picked up the picture that had always sat there, the one of the handsome man with dark, curly hair and soft brown eyes. Gently she ran her fingers around the edges of the frame and looked at it. Then she went to her closet, stretched way up on her tiptoes, and tapped at the bottom of a big, old-fashioned tin until it tumbled noisily down from the shelf.

When she put the tin on her bed and opened it, Maria and I scrambled up to look over the edges. I wasn't sure what to expect, but somehow I knew these were Mommy's treasures. Mommy lifted them out one at a time, looking each one over tenderly before replacing it again.

There was a pile of letters neatly tied with a faded ribbon, a fancy metal cigarette lighter with initials engraved on it, a baseball team shirt, a few photos of people I didn't know, and a marvelous ring with a clear stone that caught and reflected the light. "Oh!" I breathed when I saw the ring.

"I want that," Maria said, pointing at the shiny lighter.

"Who mailed you those letters?" I asked Mommy, wishing I could touch the ring.

Ignoring us, Mama slid the small picture from its frame. With shaking hands, she stuffed the ring into her blue jeans pocket. Then she sucked in a resolute breath that was sadder than any sigh I'd ever heard. She shut the picture up with the other treasures and ran into the kitchen. Maria and I followed right behind her, watching as she crammed the beautiful tin into the kitchen garbage can and then ran outside to dump it. When she came back in, she washed her hands for a long time, and I couldn't see her face. "Go get your coats on," she said suddenly, as if she'd all at once remembered we were there.

Chuck came soon after that, and Mommy loaded us into his fancy sports car. Before he started the engine, he told us the rules for passengers receiving the privilege of riding in his car. His look said more than his words. If we broke Chuck's rules, I knew his gray eyes would shoot daggers into us. When he was finished, he told us to repeat the rules back to him. We did pretty well, but he went over them once more for good measure: "Feet off the seat, butts planted, arms folded, mouths shut tight."

The ride to Nanny Julie's had never been so long. It was supposed to take only twenty minutes, but we sat on Chuck's backseat forever. As soon as the front wheels pulled into the driveway, Maria and I slid forward and touched our toes to the floor.

"Wait!" Mother commanded. "Do you remember your manners?" She reminded us in case we'd forgotten, but my thoughts had already raced through Nanny Julie's front door.

Nanny Julie and her husband had never had any children, so they liked to baby-sit us sometimes for Mommy. They had the whole house to themselves, with a big lawn, an orchard of pecan trees, a barn, and no other families close by, the way they were in our trailer court. Nanny Julie's husband was nice; he read us stories and played catch with us. But best of all, there were eight new baby kittens. Nanny Julie had promised we could hold them if we were very good, and I couldn't wait.

The instant we were free, I made a beeline for the kitties' basket. Maria and I scrambled over each other, up the back steps, and then froze in the doorway, gazing with delight. The kittens' eyes were still shut, and their weak mewing cries filled the sunny farm kitchen.

Needless to say, our two hot, dusty days with Nanny Julie whizzed by. We fed the chickens, chased the puppies, and played in the barn. Sometime after Nanny Julie bathed us and put us to bed for the second night, Mommy and Chuck came back. The hall light woke me just before I heard Mommy come in and scoop up Maria. That left Chuck for me, so I kept my eyes squeezed shut tight—I didn't want him to think I knew he was carrying me. I didn't want him ever to think I liked him.

When the sun first tickled my cheek the next morning, I threw off my covers and woke up Maria. Maria got mad—she always did. But I just hopped out of bed, and as usual, she followed right behind me into Mommy's room.

"Good morning to you," we sang, just like always. But to my absolute horror, Chuck sat up in her bed!

"Get back in your room, *now!*" he yelled at us. "And don't come out until you're called."

We ran. Maria and I sat together on my bed and cried. Finally Mama came in. She told us to stop crying and listen. "Chuck and I got married on Sunday," she said. "Chuck is your daddy now."

I'd never had a daddy before that I could remember. But I knew what one was. Daddies went to work, came home, and shared mommies' rooms. All the other kids had one. I wondered if they all thought their daddy was a yucky, scary man.

"Do you understand, Elizabeth?" Mommy was saying. Chuck had a new name now, she repeated. I was supposed to call that man Daddy.

/ / / 2 / / /

G ee, Elizabeth," Ben said in his comforting, understated way, "you look unhappy."

"Hmm?" My mind jerked back to the neat, clean lines of the empty church hallway. "Oh. Well, I was just thinking about the mothers. I mean, little children can't understand where their mothers are coming from. They only see someone who won't protect them or save them from a threat."

"Sometimes grown-up children still feel that way." He smiled, friendly creases at the corners of his eyes. "Mothers are dealing with responsibilities and expectations that a child can't understand. But sometimes they are just as confused as their children are. Sometimes they, too, endure abuse."

I wasn't looking at Ben anymore, and after that last sentence, I wasn't hearing him, either. Instead, I was recalling the words of a quotation my mother carried for years in her wallet: "The first couple of years in a marriage can be frustrating and difficult. However, with open communication between two persons . . . the ocean of erratic waves becomes a calm sea, perfect for smooth sailing."

She used to read those words softly to herself—read them often enough that I still remember them twenty-five years later, even though I didn't grasp their meaning at the time. Back then, I couldn't have understood how they burned. But I saw the flames.

"I've had it with the adjustment period!" Mama groaned one night when Daddy was working late. I was walking to my bedroom when I looked up and saw her pound her fists against the bathroom mirror. She must have thought the door was shut, but it always swung open if the latch didn't catch properly.

I stood there a moment, watching, as she leaned her head against the glass and cried. "I've had it . . . I've had it . . . " Her long auburn hair made little waving motions with each sob. Quietly I walked to her and put my hand up on her arm.

Mommy jerked around. Her face was twisted all funny, and she looked as if she was going to throw up.

"Me, too," I said. "I've had it, too." I wanted to tell her about how I felt confused and tired of all the changes in this new daddy mess. I wanted to tell her how I had been watching the other daddies on our street and how, even though they all got angry, they didn't do it as much as ours. They didn't have as many rules, either.

I wanted to put my arms around Mommy and tell her about the new feeling I had: the feeling of fear. It was a very deep terror that seemed to take over my whole body. There were times when it made me go numb, and then tingle, and then shake right down to my toes. It made my teeth hurt. My stomach and head ached as if I had the flu, but I didn't. And I figured that was how Mommy was feeling right now.

But she didn't want to talk about it.

"Elizabeth," Mama gulped and tried to find her regular voice while she reached for a tissue. "Elizabeth, where's Maria?"

"Watching 'The Bullwinkle Show.' "

"Why aren't you watching it with her? I thought that was your favorite cartoon."

"Oh, it is!" I answered. "But I don't like Boris and Natasha—especially Boris. He scares me."

"Well, run along, now," Mama said, straightening my hair with gentle fingers. "He's not real, you know. He's just a silly cartoon."

I went back in and sat down on the couch, but I didn't

really watch Bullwinkle or even Underdog. I was thinking about the first time I saw Daddy yelling at my mother. No wonder she was scared.

That morning, Mama had taken us outside to work in the yard because it was such a nice day. Then our neighbor, Mrs. Swanson, came over to visit. They talked a long time, while Maria and I tried to dam up the little stream of water flowing down the sidewalk from Mrs. Swanson's sprinklers.

Suddenly there was a squealing of tires. Daddy's GTO roared past us and hit the dip of the driveway without slowing down. He slammed on his brakes and left big, black skid marks on the cement. Then he jumped out the door and kicked it shut.

"Where have you been?" he yelled. "I've been trying to call you for the last hour!"

Mama's face went white, and so did Mrs. Swanson's. "Excuse me," Mama said to her friend. Mrs. Swanson almost ran home, and Mama was almost running, too, as Daddy put his hand on her arm and walked her inside. I took Maria away from our dam because the street is a dangerous place. We sat on the wooden steps to our house.

Daddy was yelling so loud I knew all the neighbors in the trailer park could hear him. He made two new rules that day. First, Mommy could not talk to our neighbor anymore. That woman wasn't good enough for his wife. She was poor welfare trash. Daddy said he didn't want Mommy hurting his name by spending time with low-class people like that. And second, she'd better never go anywhere without telling him first.

Then Daddy marched out the door and right past us like thunder and lightning. He drove away like that, too. He had to get back to work.

Mommy locked herself in the bathroom after that. She took a bath. But we could hear her crying, even though the water was running and the radio was singing.

In the years since, I have heard people use the phrase "green with envy." But green isn't the right color. Jealousy is a deep, fiery red that is sometimes purple and sometimes white-hot in the center. And that was about the right color for Daddy.

What happened that day didn't upset me so very much—but he did. His words weren't naughty or bad ones, but they were ugly. His voice was different. He said everything in an evil tone that pierced every part of my body. It was a tone I knew I would never forget.

/ / / / /

"There are variables," Ben was saying. "Violence is one thing that has a significant impact on how lasting the effects of abuse are."

"Violence isn't always physical," I said, remembering to keep up the conversation. "There can be verbal violence, too." I was still hearing echoes of that tone in Daddy's voice. "And the only thing that could be worse than seeing your mother mistreated would be having it happen to you."

/ / / / /

I remembered an evening when twilight had just begun to settle across the neighborhood. The street lights were blinking on, and the dinner was cleared away. Maria had wandered off to play with her doctor kit, but I scooted a stool up to the counter beside Mama. She'd been making a lemon pie, and now it was time to put the meringue on it.

Using her new mixer, Mama beat the egg whites she'd already separated from the yolks. It took a long time, but at last they were tall and fluffy, like clouds way up in the sky. Mommy's fingers looked long and slender and so very graceful as she swirled the meringue across the top of the pie. She could make it do beautiful things. Her pies looked like the ones in bakery windows that people took home in boxes. And when her creation was finished, she held it high in the air to inspect her work.

"Oh!" she exclaimed. "I forgot to heat the oven. Here, Liz," she said, moving the stool I was standing on away from the oven and turning it on. I don't know if she realized it, but she had scooted me right in front of that delicious-looking, fluffy meringue.

Mama scooped up the bowl and beaters and took them over

to the sink to wash them. Suddenly I had an urge—an irresistible urge—to find out what that beautiful white stuff tasted like.

My mouth watering in anticipation, I stretched onto my tip-toes and leaned against the counter, my chin in the palms of my hands. My entire concentration was locked on the masterpiece before me until, finally, I reached out one finger, scooped up the tiniest bit, and popped it into my mouth.

"No!" Daddy screeched. "No! No! No!" He'd been watching me from the living room, and he marched into the kitchen. "Never!"

Angrily, he hunted through the kitchen drawers, shuffling the contents, and then slamming them shut. All the while he yelled at me about pigs and germs.

Mommy froze, her hands motionless in the soapy water. I couldn't help myself—I started to cry. Then he grabbed me and tied my hands behind my back with a piece of string he'd found. With one smooth motion he lifted the pie and dumped it onto the floor. The next instant he was forcing me to my knees over the pie, shoving my face down into the sticky heap that had been Mama's marvelous creation.

"You want to be a pig?" he shouted in my ear. "You're now a pig. *Eat!*"

I sobbed my guts out. No four-year-old can eat a whole pie, no matter how delicious it is. And after my first stolen snitch, this one tasted like gooey slime. But whenever I choked or gagged or even slowed a little, he screamed at me again. His big hand came down hard and plastered my face into the mess.

Eventually there was nothing left but sweet stickiness smeared across the floor, and I thought my ordeal was over. But I was wrong. He leaned over me and shouted again, "Lick up the rest. Pigs, even dogs, lick their platters clean!"

I began licking. With each new effort, I thought I would lose everything. But my fear kept me from that. What would he do if I threw up all over? I didn't want to find out. He was way too angry; the evil tone completely filled his voice.

/ / / / /

"Why do women stay in situations like that?" I asked out loud. "If it's so horrible, why don't they get out? If they won't do it for themselves, then why not for their children?"

Years before I had come up with a list of insights and speculations to dissipate my own anger. The pain was very real, but I had worked at letting go of the anger. At that moment, I was curious what Ben thought. Without the anger clouding my vision, I could try to understand his response, but there had been a time when anything he said would have made no sense at all.

I began to think that maybe I really was a pig for snitching. When I was four, I began to learn that I had many flaws. I couldn't concentrate all the time, and sometimes I forgot a rule— or, more accurately, I got sidetracked.

That was a sin. I knew it because I spent hours in a corner with my nose firmly against the wall. I spent days in my room. And I received many spankings with a wide variety of tools: wooden spoons that eventually broke, hangers that soon bent out of shape, and big belts that stung bare skin. Once when I was being punished, Daddy's swinging belt shattered the light fixture on the ceiling, and so I got two extra lashings because of it. I also got to clean up the broken glass. It cut my fingers, but bad girls don't get Band-Aids.

Then came the night my mother whispered through her teeth, "Go get your jammies. Quick! And bring Maria's, too."

I ran. Something was up. I knew because she was whispering, but I couldn't guess what it was. When I went back into her room, I saw her travel bag open on her bed. Her nightgown was already in it, and so was a change of clothes for us girls.

Mama didn't take time to fold anything. She threw in a pair of pants and a shirt for herself, along with our three toothbrushes, and then shut and locked the travel bag. Grabbing the leather handles in one hand, she took both our little ones in the other and hurried out the front door.

We walked right past Daddy's truck in the driveway. He'd taken the GTO, but that didn't matter because Mama didn't have keys to either one. She just kept walking determinedly down the sidewalk.

"Where are we going?" I asked in a stage whisper. Little Maria's feet couldn't go fast enough, so Mommy swung her up and carried her for a while.

"Shhh! Just come quick, Elizabeth."

After a couple of blocks she set Maria down, and we two ran right ahead of her. She kept looking back over her shoulder toward our house.

I didn't know where we were running, but I knew why. Earlier that afternoon Daddy had tried teaching Mommy to ride her new horse. The week before, he'd bought a strong quarter horse for himself and a tall palomino for Mommy. And best of all, he'd arranged to stable them at Nanny Julie's. Maria and I loved playing around the barn and pasture and sneaking into Nanny Julie's for a cookie or two. But today hadn't been so much fun.

Mama had not been able to make her horse behave, so Daddy yelled and yelled at her. He was good with horses—or at least he thought he was. "Show 'im who's boss, Maureen. Take control!"

Mama was very pale, and her hands were shaking. She kept brushing one hand across her forehead, even though her hair hadn't slipped out of the neat bun she'd twisted at the back of her neck. Again and again, Mommy bit at her lip and jerked the reins in a determined way, but the horse was much stronger than she was. When her horse bolted against her will and ran into the barn for the third time, she climbed down and cried, "I give up!"

Daddy was even angrier now. He grabbed a whip from one of the tack rooms and mounted Mommy's horse. Then he began kicking and hitting the palomino's fair hide.

Mommy took Maria and me by the hand and pulled us into Daddy's truck. The dust rose in the hot air, as Daddy made the palomino turn and wheel, race and stop short. When he was tired, he unsaddled the sweaty, foaming horse. He threw the saddles and bits and blankets into the back of the truck and then grabbed us girls and tossed us into the back as well.

Through the cab window, we could see Daddy yelling and yelling and yelling at Mommy. Tears were streaming down her face, and she didn't have any tissues. The wind whipped us all the way home.

That was why we were running away. I don't think I usually could have walked so far, but this was different from any normal situation.

Mama checked us into a small motel. Maria and I had never been in a motel before, but we knew right off they were nice. There was a big bed, a TV, a bathroom, and a telephone. What an adventure! Mommy said we were going to watch TV in bed together.

I think she wanted to watch with us, but she was nervous. She kept walking up and down the floor. Maria and I wanted to enjoy the nice color TV, too, but it was hard not to watch Mommy. Finally she plopped down on the edge of the bed and picked up the phone.

She called Daddy! I was outraged. They talked for a while, and then Mommy hung up. The fun was soon going to be over, I knew. Daddy would spoil everything.

When he knocked on the door, Mommy stepped outside. After a while, she came in and picked up her travel bag. We were going back, with him.

/ / / 3 / / /

W hy do women stay in situations like that?" Ben repeated
my question back to me. After a pause, he spoke slowly, thinking his way through the answer as he went. "I'm
not sure, Elizabeth. Most often they feel trapped. Sometimes
they don't realize the extent of the abuse their children face.
Certainly, their own self-esteem is hurt by the abuse. But even
then, they may counteract their feelings of worthlessness by
playing the role of martyr. They feel it would be wrong to hurt
the abuser; they feel he needs them."

"That's noble," I said, meaning it. "But sometimes people
need to consider the price and be sure someone else isn't also
paying for their merciful feelings. Besides," I added, shifting my
Relief Society materials to my other arm, "being a doormat isn't
really doing the abuser any favors, either."

Ben grinned. "Nope, you're right. But most of the time I
don't think these wives and mothers realize they're perpetuating the problem. They're on the defensive, feeling trapped.
Remember, their own self-esteem has been battered. They may
not think they can face the world alone. Being a single mother
can be an immense, almost superhuman burden. With that staring them in the face, they keep trying to make things work."

/ / / / /

Ben was right about that. After many months passed, my

mother seemed to feel things were at least somewhat better. The truth is, we had all learned how to walk on eggshells.

August came after I turned five. That made this year special. Mama was sewing and snipping and ironing for days. She made dresses with ribbons and crinoline, dresses with lacy pinafores. Every one had rows of ruffles.

My job was to keep quiet and play with Maria until Mommy called me to try something on or help her stretch it out. I had to be very careful because the pieces often had pins in them.

My other job was to practice my alphabet, count to ten, and repeat our telephone number and address. I wasn't sure why that was important, but my upcoming adventure depended on it. Anticipation was making me bounce on the inside of every inch of my body.

One day it was all I could do to stay under control. We were going shopping after Daddy came home. The hours passed as slowly as a cactus grows, but he finally drove up and we all jumped into his truck.

"Kinney's is the best place to buy children's shoes," he told Mama, so we went to Kinney's.

When we walked into the store, Mommy reminded us to use our manners, but Daddy went even further by telling us to sit down, fold our arms, and not move. Except for turning our heads to gawk all around, we sat like statues.

Mommy and Daddy picked up shoe after shoe, looking each one over, always putting them down. Daddy picked up one that was made of black patent leather. My heart jumped when he held that shiny shoe up in the light.

Please oh please oh please . . . , my insides were pleading.

Then the salesman began talking to Daddy, and he put that lovely shoe down. The salesman went away and came back with four boxes in his arms.

"My, what nice young ladies," he said to us. "Can you take your own shoes off?"

"You bet!" I answered, as Maria and I began pulling frantically at our laces. "Have you got anything in there for her, too?"

I asked hopefully. "Maria's been feeling sad because she doesn't get to go to school next week like I do."

"Hmmm." The chubby salesman pulled a serious expression. He opened the top box and took out a pair of red Keds. "Do you think these might work?"

"Oh yes!" Maria's dark, round eyes were as bright as the sun while he laced them onto her feet. She walked around the floor, gazing in all the low mirrors. Daddy pinched her toe, and then the salesman did it, too.

"Those will do," Daddy said.

The salesman looked at me and grinned, "So you're starting kindergarten next week, huh, carrot-top?"

"Yep," I answered, looking hopefully at the unopened boxes. "Sure am." My heart pounded as he took off the first lid. *Oh please oh please . . .*

Inside was a pair of Keds like Maria's, but they were plain black. I tried to smile and look happy when they told me to walk around. Daddy and the salesman pinched my toes.

The salesman was nice. "Come see what else your father has chosen," he said. He took off the other lid, uncovering a pair of brown dress shoes with buckles. I walked around again, while everyone said how sturdy they were. Then he opened another box, pulled the brown shoes off my feet, and said, "Push."

"Oh!" I squealed, looking down. He was putting those patent leather beauties on my feet!

"You like these, huh?" he chuckled.

Daddy leaned over and pinched my toes again. "We'll take these and the two pair of Keds," he said importantly.

I wanted to dance all over the floor. Maria and I hugged each other. Daddy thanked the salesman and then let Mommy carry the boxes out. My imagination soared away into visions of ruffles and lace and shiny patent leather. But when we were climbing into his truck, Daddy took both my arms and whirled me around to face him.

"The shiny shoes are school shoes. They will *never* be worn at any other time," he said in a low, frightening voice. "The tennis shoes are the ones you may play in. You will shine your leather shoes every day and keep them in their box. Do you understand?"

"Oh, yes, sir!" I answered, remembering my manners. "Yes . . . and thank you."

"And one more thing," he said sternly, almost accusingly. "I've spent a lot of money on material, coats, galoshes, and new shoes. If I ever catch you not taking care of your things, you'll be going to school naked—and that's a promise!" He let go of my arms. "I work too hard for you to waste my money."

Kindergarten morning finally arrived. Mama spent a long time curling my hair before she let me choose my favorite new dress. By the time she was through, I was all done up in a green calico print with a frilly white pinafore, white lacy anklets, and my black patent leather shoes.

Lifting me up onto the bathroom counter, Mommy said, "Well, what do you think?"

I looked into the mirror. Dancing green eyes and a big smile filled up my freckled face. Framing all this were the bobbing, symmetrical, carrot-red ringlets Mommy had worked so hard to perfect.

"Are you happy, angel?" Mommy asked, putting her arms around me.

I squeezed her back excitedly.

"Let's go now, before you're late." Lifting me down, Mommy scooped up my book bag, took Maria's hand, and walked us a long way down the street to the school.

Kindergarten was every bit as wonderful as I'd ever dreamed. The teacher, Mrs. Edwards, was firm, but her eyes and her smile were marvelously kind. We each had our own coat hook, cubbyhole, and desk with our name on it. Playtime and recess and singing time and—oh! It was all fantastically exciting.

School was an entirely new world for me. Right away I understood that it was a much safer place than home. In the classroom I could try new things. Activities and ideas that I would have been afraid to try at home were at my fingertips here. This was a place for discovery.

Actually, that was the first thing Mrs. Edwards explained to us when we were all finally settled into our desks that exciting afternoon. Kindergarten, she said, was a place to learn. At school you were supposed to learn things, try out new stuff, ask questions. And it didn't take me long to realize that through my interactions with her and with the other children, I was going to learn a lot.

Well into the school year, after the rainy season had hit Arizona, I was walking home with my two best friends. The weatherman had said there might be a storm, but instead, the desert sun was blazing like July all over again. About two blocks from the school, we came upon something that made us all stop walking at once. Our chatter broke off as we smiled at each other with eager delight.

All the lawns in that block were kept green by sprinklers, and here was a house where an automatic system had goofed. The front lawn was entirely submerged under three inches of water!

"Let's hold hands and jump together!" Lonnie whispered.

"Wait a minute," I said, dropping to the sidewalk and pulling my galoshes out of my school bag. "I don't dare get my shoes wet."

"Who cares?" Carrie asked. "Come on!"

But I knew better than to let her talk me out of it. I tugged those galoshes over my shoes, and even though anticipation made me clumsy, I finally got them hooked. "On your mark!" I hollered, as we teetered, holding hands on the edge of the sidewalk.

"Get set!" Lonnie yelled. We all bent our knees in eagerness. Carrie sucked in a deep breath. *"Go!"*

We jumped. We danced. We sang. And the water went up in a sun-catching rainbow spray all around us. Deliciously cool on that hot sunny afternoon, it splattered down on us like a private rainstorm.

Honk! Honk!

Lonnie and Carrie kept singing, but I froze.

Honk! Honnnnnnk! Daddy's truck was pulled up beside the opposite curb. Lonnie and Carrie quit dancing and were looking at me. I couldn't move. I just kept staring at Daddy and Mommy and Maria, who were staring back at me.

Mommy got out of the truck and led me across the street. She lifted me into the back. Nobody said anything until we were inside the house. Then Daddy gave me a very mean beating with a wooden spoon. The hitting seemed to go on forever. On and on. I lost count of the lickings. I lost track of everything, except my behind, which stung as if it were bleeding. When he finally finished, Daddy told me the beating was for "trespassing." Then, for being late, he added a "groundation period" on top of it. For two weeks I was to sit in the corner of my bedroom in my rocking chair. I could only leave that spot to go to school and to the bathroom, to eat my meals, and to sleep in my bed. During those two weeks, Mommy was never going to come into my room.

I could hardly sit. Curled over on my hip, I sobbed myself to sleep in the chair. Why had Mommy let Daddy hit me so hard? So very, very hard?

The next morning I met Lonnie and Carrie as they were walking to school. I told them what had happened to me and asked them what their punishments were. To my absolute amazement, Lonnie had escaped the event without even a scolding. Carrie had been given a warning always to come straight home after school and not to dilly-dally ever again.

"You mean your daddy didn't give you beatings?" I asked, stupefied. We were walking past the lawn where we'd danced the afternoon before. Just looking at all that damp green grass made me shudder.

"My daddy disciplines the boys, and my mother disciplines the girls," Carrie said in a matter-of-fact way.

"Discipline?" I asked. "What's that?"

"Oh, that just means we have to do some work. However bad we are, that's how hard the work is."

"Do you get disciplined, too?" I asked Lonnie.

"I dunno," Lonnie said, smiling her toothless grin. "My mommy yells a lot, and sometimes my daddy gives us spankings, but I never have to do work."

"What does he use?" I asked. "I mean, what does your daddy spank with?" I was thinking of spoons and hangers and straps and belts and wondering how Lonnie could be smiling about this.

"He uses his hand, silly. That's how you give spankings."

I was shocked.

Lonnie was still smiling. "Wanna hear a secret?"

"Yeah!" Carrie and I chorused.

"Well, when I'm in trouble, I just give my mom the 'silent treatment.' "

"The what?"

"The 'silent treatment.' " We were almost to the school, so we slowed our steps and Lonnie spoke in a whispery voice. "That's when you don't talk to anybody until you get what you want."

"Do they think you're real sad or something?" Carrie asked as the first bell sounded.

"I guess," Lonnie giggled. "You ought to try it, Elizabeth. Maybe you can get out of your groundation period."

I will, I thought, walking up the front steps and into class with my friends. *I'll show Mommy.*

When I walked through the back door after school, Mama looked up from her ironing with a smile, just like always. "Hello, 'Lizbeth. How was school?"

Ignoring her, I stiffened my back, put my nose in the air, and marched straight into my room.

As usual, Maria followed me, her mouth going like a speedboat. "What'd ya do today, Liz? What'd ya do?"

"Shhh!" I hissed. "I'm not talking tonight. I'm doing the 'silent treatment,' so go away."

Maria was disappointed. She looked at me for a long moment and then went back into the front room where she'd been watching cartoons.

Hours went by. I wondered how long this was going to take. I hummed to myself, carefully, quietly, so that no one could hear me. I imagined all the neat things I ought to be doing outside right then. I would have given up on the "treatment" working, but there was no chance to talk to anyone, anyway. So I just sat there alone, far away in my imagination.

Finally (it was after dark!), Daddy came in and sat down on my bed. His voice was low, but it wasn't kind or penitent. "Mom says she thinks you've been punished enough. She says you've been real quiet, and she thinks you're real sorry." He tipped my face up and looked into it. "Are you *real* sorry?"

I nodded.

"Okay, I'll let you off this time. But it had better never happen again."

I was getting ready to run away to freedom when he grabbed my arm.

"Do you hear me?"

I nodded again. "Yes, sir."

Daddy got up and stomped out of the room ahead of me.

As soon as he was gone, I raised my fist to the sky and silently gave a deafening cheer: *Yes! It worked! ALL RIGHT!*

/ / / **4** / / /

I t was a beautiful house. That's what I remember best about it: the beauty. From the rail fence along the front sidewalk to the flowers out in back, I loved our new little house. The yard stretched beyond the patio, beneath the fruit trees, out into the flower and vegetable gardens.

Mixing ourselves in with all this beauty, I thought things would change. With all the modest, pretty charm around us, surely our relationships would modify themselves to match. Even my old bed felt different to sleep in.

But everything was really the same.

Mother was in love with her cozy little home, and Daddy was proud. He was the provider. He kept saying he'd finally arrived. He'd just purchased himself a house, a house he would share with Maureen, a house that he would let Maureen's two little girls live in. But of course, there would be rules. There were always rules. And if we didn't keep them, we would be sent to the toolshed.

The toolshed! my heart cried. *Why does everything nice have a dark, scary cloud hovering over it?*

Rules, rules, rules. Before long, Maria and I wondered just how many rules there could be. I certainly couldn't seem to keep track of them all, let alone complete all of the chores I was required to do each day. I spent most of my days grounded in my room, for it seemed that I could never do my jobs well enough to please Daddy.

Each mistake cost me my freedom, my play, my television, and my phone privileges for two weeks. The "silent treatment" didn't work very often after I first used it, and as one two-week period piggybacked onto another during the next three years, my life became increasingly unhappy. There was a deep ache growing within me that no one seemed to notice or care about.

But there was one thing that was never taken from me: school. That was the only place where I could escape and enjoy things. In the face of all that was discouraging about my life and my apparent incompetence, people at school seemed to like me. My teachers said I was doing well in my studies, and I had plenty of friends in my classes. As kindergarten gave way to first, second, and then third grade, I clung to school as if it were the life raft keeping me alive.

/ / / / /

Our blue Buick pulled up just outside the church door, and my mind jumped back to the present. Darren was here for me now. But right along with that thought came two others.

First, he would come in and look for me, so I didn't have to hurry away. Darren hadn't seen Ben in a long time, and I wanted him to have a chance to say hello, too.

Second, I thought of the discussion we'd had the night before. I'd just been in and kissed the golden heads of my sleeping children. (They're such quick-tanning blonds like their father that when their round green eyes are closed you almost can't see me in them.) When I went into our bedroom, I briefly related to Darren an unpleasant incident that had happened to our son at Scouts that day. "I just hope he can forget it," I worried.

"Oh, he will," Darren answered gently. When I was silent, he added, "Of course he will. Children don't remember every little thing that happens to them. It all gets lost as the years pour over their lives."

"Yes," I said, "that's true, but certain things stick out so clearly you can't forget."

Darren caught the tone in my voice, and he put his arms around me. "Most children forget, Elizabeth." His voice was soft and understanding. We'd been over this ground so many times before that he was quick to recognize my need for reassurance. "You remember things vividly because of the circumstances you grew up in. But Ryan's situation is different. We've committed ourselves to making it that way."

Darren's insight was good. Remembering had been a survival skill for me because forgetting might mean repeating a mistake, and I paid dearly for each of those.

But my children's lives are different. They don't lie awake in the darkness, coping with feelings of fear and insecurity. Although my past will never fade away as if it hadn't happened, my husband and I can choose, and we have decided to make things better for our children. Together, with God's help, Darren and I are breaking the chains of abuse rather than passing dysfunction and emotional sickness on to shackle our little ones.

As I thought about these things, standing there in the church hallway, a warm feeling rushed around me. I felt as secure as I'd felt in my husband's arms the night before. I was so grateful for Darren, for his patience, for his love.

But from where Ben was standing, he couldn't see Darren, and he didn't know my thoughts. He was still smiling at me in his relaxed way that allowed us to pursue our own thoughts while we talked.

And so my mind went on skipping rapidly, like a rock across water. With each bounce I caught another glimpse of the past: a memory, skip up into fresh air, a memory, skip up again and make a comment, another memory. . . .

/　/　/　/　/

There was a new feeling around our house one day. It had been building all week, but on Wednesday it had grown so big that it couldn't be ignored. Daddy was being very sweet. In fact, he was so sweet my stomach churned with worry. Something was up—I knew by the painful lump in my throat and the gut-wrenching nervousness that warned me whenever there was trouble.

That may sound like a cliché, but it really wasn't. By the time I was nine, I had begun to rely heavily on my feelings. Hunches were my best friends. If I listened to the quiet, it never lied to me.

Mama was in a particularly good mood that day, too. She was busy in the kitchen when I came home, fixing tacos with homemade tortillas and fresh picante sauce and guacamole, everybody's favorite. I set the table as usual and then went to play with Maria. But the smell of garlic and cilantro was just too much. Soon all of us—even Daddy—were hanging around the kitchen door waiting for the call to eat.

When everything was finally ready, Maria and I nearly ran to our chairs. But Daddy cleared his throat before taking a bite of his dinner. "There's something very important that we all need to talk about," he said, with a grin on his lips and a twinkle in his eye. I looked closer at him. It wasn't his expression that startled me so much, though. This was the first time I could ever remember his voice being shaky.

"Something very important," he repeated, clearing his throat again and looking at our mother. "I've gotten permission from the courts," he took her hand in his and then turned and looked at Maria and me. "And now I need your permission for something."

What was he talking about? Since when had he ever asked our permission for anything?

"I want to adopt you," Daddy said.

My mind suddenly went nuts. Adopt us! I'd always known he wasn't my real dad, but I'd never dared sort out my relationship with him before. My mind blundered around, somewhat paralyzed by this subject that no one had ever discussed.

Long ago, when Daddy had first begun hanging around, I'd known that he wasn't the same man who'd gone away to the Vietnam War. That man was really my father. I'd heard Mama tell someone that Maria got her dark eyes and I got my pretty singing voice from him. That man's picture had been on Mama's nightstand until the weekend she had gone away to Nevada with Chuck to get married. And there were the days just before kindergarten when Mommy had told me my last name was O'Brien, not Hughes like hers.

"I'm sure you both know I'm not your real dad," he went on persuasively. "But if I adopt you, I will legally be your father, and you can use my name."

My mind was beyond clear thinking or carefulness. "If you adopt us, will that mean you finally like us?"

Daddy's face turned red.

"Elizabeth!" my mother shrieked.

I ducked. I thought for sure he would hit me for blurting out like that.

Maria was beaming. "He must love us, now, 'Lizbeth," she chimed with sweet eagerness. "He must, or those court men wouldn't let him adopt us."

"What makes those courts think you love us?" I was keeping my distance, stunned.

Daddy looked at us with an empty face. "Because I do love you both," he said at last. He went on, his words running out into the chaos of my thoughts. "If I didn't love you I wouldn't be here. I wouldn't buy you food or nice things or let you live in my house."

"Oh," I answered softly.

Daddy kept talking about all the things he let us have, things that were supposed to be proof of his love. But my mind had run far away. I was already planning, rationalizing, hoping.

If Maria and I said yes, then everything would be legal. I wasn't sure how important legal was, but it sounded serious and respectable. The courts must have believed that he loved us enough to want to be our dad. He must have promised to be very good. Surely the courts knew that he wasn't always good; courts must have investigators who find out about everything. That must have been why he had been extra nice for the last few days. Maybe he really had promised to be good.

I wondered if Hughes was easier to spell than O'Brien. I

knew it had been hard for Maria to learn how to spell that. I looked over at her.

Maria's big eyes were even wider than usual. She was looking at me, and I knew she was wanting me to make a decision. She usually agreed to whatever I decided on things. I closed my eyes and took a deep breath.

Daddy was still talking, but I just said, "Yes." Maybe this would somehow make things better.

Daddy stopped talking suddenly. By the silence I knew he was waiting, listening, so I said it again.

"Yes."

/ / / / /

"Have you noticed how much more we've been hearing through the media about sexual abuse lately?" Ben was saying. "It must look like a lot of people are anxious to find a complaint forum, an attention-bandwagon to jump on. But I've treated enough individuals in my medical practice and counseled with enough ward members to know it is a very real problem. And unfortunately, it's far more prevalent than most of us realize."

"You're right," I said. "We do seem to bump into it everywhere these days. I never heard anyone talk about abuse or incest when I was small. At least, not until the general conference when President Monson spoke directly about the problem."

"I've been gathering information in case I ever do write a book," Ben said. "And I have a copy of that statement right here in my calendar. I keep it handy because it's critical for someone who was molested as a child to understand that what happened was not the child's fault."

"What exactly did he say, again?" I asked, wanting to hear those words that had been so helpful to me.

"Well," Ben said earnestly, "President Monson didn't deal very tenderly with perpetrators. He said, 'Liars, bullies who abuse children, they will one day reap the whirlwind of their foul deeds.' "

That's a good start, I thought, waiting for him to go on.

"Then he mentioned a letter he had received from a district judge. Apparently the judge had said that 'sexual abuse of children is one of the most depraved, destructive, and demoralizing crimes in civilized society. There is an alarming increase of reported physical, psychological, and sexual abuse of children. Our courts are becoming inundated with this repulsive behavior.' " Ben paused and drew a deep breath. "It does seem to be a sickening flood all around us."

Washing right over some of us, I thought.

"President Monson went on to make what I consider to be an official statement of the Church's position. He said: 'The Church does not condone such heinous and vile conduct. Rather, we condemn in the harshest of terms such treatment of God's precious children. Let the child be rescued, nurtured, loved, and healed. Let the offender be brought to justice, to accountability, for his actions and receive professional treatment to curtail such wicked and devilish conduct.' "[1]

Wicked. Devilish. Yes, I couldn't think of better words to describe such flagrant violation of someone else's agency.

"Ben, are you familiar with Moroni 9:9?" I asked.

"The passage where the Nephites deprived the Lamanites' daughters of 'that which was most dear and precious above all things'?"

"Yes, that's it." I was surprised he knew—but then, maybe he *had* been serious about writing a book. "Yes, 'chastity and virtue.' "

He nodded.

"Well," I stopped. "I can't think of a worse thing anyone could do." The hall was awfully quiet. My words were hanging with tremulous intensity, so I added, "Of course, we're told there's one worse sin: murder. But I'm sure it's a lot easier to be dead than to deal with the torment of having lost that most precious possession, especially before even understanding what it is."

NOTE

1. Thomas S. Monson, "Precious Children—A Gift from God," *Ensign,* Nov. 1991, p. 69.

/ / / 5 / / /

Things should have been pretty good during that long, dry summer when I turned nine. We lived in a wonderful little house and, once the judge had banged his heavy gavel, we were officially a "real" family.

The school year seemed to have paid attention to the calendar but not to the seasons. Blazing desert sunshine held the days in its grip long after the rainy season had usually begun. My friends all wished they could still be hanging around the swimming pool, but I was grateful that school had come back into my life.

One Thursday afternoon I was busy with my usual after-school chores. As I carried the kitchen garbage out to the trash cans behind the garage, I began thinking about that day's math test and wondering whether or not I'd gotten the eighth question right. I dumped the trash and started back for the bathroom's wastebasket, walking around the toolshed built onto the back of the garage and toward the back door.

"Come in here," Daddy said to me from the doorway of the toolshed.

I followed him to where he sat down on his workbench, beneath the window. He picked up a magazine that was lying open on the jigsaw table.

"I hear you saw a special film at school."

"Yes," I said. Actually, we'd seen two that day, one in science

36

and one in health class. The movie in science had been about volcanoes, showing hot, red lava pouring down mountainsides, knocking over trees, hissing and burning. The other film had been about the changes girls' bodies make as they become young women. We'd all been giggling and teasing about who would be a late bloomer. At nine those things are still a few years off, which is pretty much the same as forever.

"Well, I thought we should discuss it." Daddy's voice had a tone I'd never heard before; there was a look in his eyes I wasn't familiar with.

Something inside me clicked, and I began to feel very uneasy—not just a little uneasy, but awfully, sickeningly uneasy. A voice inside me whispered, "Run!"

What was I to run from? Where was I to go?

"As you go through puberty, Elizabeth, not only will you change on the outside but you will be changing on the inside."

Now I knew which filmstrip he meant. The room seemed to be shrinking in size. Suddenly it felt dark. Fear washed over me in a wave. How could I run? I was trapped.

"You've probably noticed those changes already." He put his hand on my arm and tried to lock my eyes with his. "The changes, Elizabeth? They're called hormones. You've probably noticed them already."

My mind was dull. I couldn't—I didn't want to—understand what he was talking about.

"Hormones." He repeated the word, and I thought it sounded nasty. "Do you know what I mean?" He squeezed my arm tighter.

"No."

"Well, let me help you." He let go of my arm and flipped through the magazine. Stopping, he held it up for me to look.

It was a naked man.

I glanced away. Why was he showing me this? The boys saw pictures like that in their health class, I supposed, but all we saw was a film on girls becoming young women. They wouldn't have divided us if we were supposed to see each other's stuff.

"How does that picture make your body feel?"

My heart was pounding. I was sure I was going to throw up. Why couldn't I just disappear or waste away? What should I say? I was afraid to make him angry. Where was Mom? Where was Maria?

His question never fully registered in my mind. Instead of answering, I heard myself spit out the words, "I DON'T WANT TO TALK ABOUT THESE THINGS WITH YOU!"

"Well, maybe not yet," he chuckled, "but you'd better think about it." When he chuckled, I felt embarrassed and dirty. "Hormones don't go away." He placed the magazine on the bench in front of me and walked out of the shed.

I just stood there, frozen in my shoes. Numb and cold.

/   /   /   /   /

Ben was smiling at me patiently. There was a compassionate light in his eyes.

I looked away with a sinking feeling. *What if he knows?*

Although it was awful, my past isn't a locked secret. Yet I'd tried to put it behind me long ago. When I think of myself, I don't immediately think *victim of abuse.* There was a time when that was the biggest part of my identity. Now I see myself first as *Elizabeth:* wife, mother, friend, Relief Society worker, PTA room parent, and so on.

I didn't want Ben to think of me as someone who needed his pity. I didn't want him to see me as a woman who had been soiled long ago, dirtied with such a deep, dark stain that she might never quite be emotionally ironed out. What I wanted was his continued friendship, understanding, and respect.

Drawing a deep breath, I looked back again at my friend.

There was nothing to worry about. Maybe it came from something in his casual dress and attitude, but it seemed to be deeper than his manner, something more. He was unpretentious. He knew who he was, and he accepted and liked me for who I was, too.

Suddenly I realized that if he guessed, it was okay. I didn't mind if he knew about my struggles. He could be trusted. There *are* some people worth trusting. Ben was one of them, and so was Darren.

If only I'd known them twenty years ago.

/ / / / /

I was raking grass clippings in our backyard. Lawn cleanup was a standard item on my list of chores, and I was pretty good at it. Not many nine-year-old girls can rake swiftly, aggressively, and pretend to be riding their bike at the same time.

"Elizabeth."

I jumped. Maybe I wasn't as clever as I thought.

"Come in here a minute," Daddy said.

After knocking the clippings from the tines of my rake, I propped it against the little eucalyptus tree Daddy had recently planted and followed him into the toolshed. I hadn't been in there since the last time he'd asked me to come in, and I was deeply relieved as he walked past his workbench toward the other side of the low, slanting room.

The toolshed had been one of our house's big selling points for Daddy. Bigger than most other sheds, it stretched across the entire width of the two-car garage. He led me to where his athletic equipment was organized on some shelves and hooks against the far wall. There, shoved back into a dark corner, was a big metal tool chest.

Pushing down hard on the top, he flipped the latch open with his thumb. He burrowed into the chest, tossing out a pair of jumper cables, some bungee cords, a jack, and a wrench. With a grunt of satisfaction, Daddy pulled out a stack of magazines and dropped them into my arms.

"Hold these," he commanded in a businesslike way.

As he began stuffing things back into the chest, I looked down at the load in my arms. The picture of a near-naked woman leaped up at me from the front cover.

My stomach lurched, and I mentally dropped the stack as if it were on fire. But in reality my arms could not move. *Please, not again,* I silently pleaded.

Run, the little voice inside me insisted. *Run!*

Where? Where could I run? How could I get away from Daddy when Mama and Maria were gone?

"Maybe this will give you an idea of what the new you is going to look like," Daddy said, leaning over me. I could feel his breath hot on my cheek and the scent of his cologne made me queasy. But he didn't notice. He seemed to think he had important knowledge that I was secretly dying for him to share. "We also need to finish discussing what we started the other day. You need to get in touch with your feelings so you will understand them. If you don't understand them, you can't learn to handle them."

That new, disgusting tone of voice and the ugly, nasty look had completely taken over his face. He chuckled again as he added, "And hormones can be difficult to handle."

As he talked, Daddy thumbed through the magazine, occasionally stopping to stare at the naked bodies, trying to get me to look at them, too. When he reached the centerfold, he kicked the lid of the tool chest shut and spread the picture out on top. "You see, Frecklie-frog" (he said that nickname as if it would endear him to me), "your hormones control the feelings you get whenever you're around someone of the opposite sex."

Quickly he grabbed another magazine and thumbed through it to a picture of a naked man. He put that picture next to the one of the naked woman.

The same revulsion I'd felt before flooded over me in overwhelming waves. I was trapped again. Daddy kept on asking questions and making me answer. He was standing right behind me now and pressing me against the tool chest, his fingers digging deep into my shoulders.

I couldn't get away. Hot, humiliated tears stung my eyes.

The little voice inside me was still urging me, *Run! Run! Run now!* it screamed.

As he began to move his hands down from my shoulders, he loosened his grip ever so slightly. That was when I twisted away.

"You're gross!" I shouted as I ran. I ran all the way to my bedroom and slammed the door. I didn't dare to look back; I just slumped down on the edge of my bed.

Don't come in, don't come in! my heart pleaded. How I wished my door locked from the inside.

Then, suddenly, terror engulfed me as I heard the back door slam. My heart stopped—I couldn't breathe as his footsteps came up the stairs and down the hall. My skin crawled. I bit my lip. He opened a door, but it wasn't mine, It was his, across the hall.

I drew a deep breath as another flood of nausea washed over me. Now I was in trouble for sure. He would be mad. I should never have yelled at him.

What could I do? Sitting there, waiting for what might happen, was impossible. I'd better hurry and do my chores again, make sure each one was perfect. He'd be watching for me to make a mistake, so he could punish me good.

Why doesn't Mama come home? I wondered as I tiptoed to my bedroom door. I swallowed hard, pushing aside the fear of what might happen when I left my room.

As I swung my door open, the door across the hall began to open, too. I hurried, but I got only as far as the top of the stairs.

"Elizabeth."

My heart jumped, hammered, stuck in my throat. "Yes, sir?" I said, turning around. He was standing there, right in front of me—naked.

I looked down at the varnished floorboards beneath my feet. That was the first time I'd ever seen my Daddy without his clothes on.

"Where are you going?"

"I . . . I'm going t . . . t' do m-m-my chores," I answered, my eyes locked on the parallel boards.

"All right." He turned and went back into his room, closing the door behind him.

I thought I was going to pass out right there, but my feet went racing away, down the stairs. *What was he trying to do?* The question whirled through my mind, too big for me to stifle. *How can I get this to stop?*

Later that evening, Daddy drove out to the stables to care for his horses. As soon as he was gone, I told my mother everything that had happened, in detail.

She showed about as much emotion as a brick wall. "I'm sorry," Mom said at last. "Don't worry about it," she added without any inflection in her voice. "I'll talk to him."

I was amazed. She didn't seem to care at all—and I'd expected her to be furious. Didn't Mom believe me? She'd always trusted me before. *Please . . . please, she's GOT to believe me!*

/ / / / /

"There you are, Liz!" Darren said, bursting happily through the foyer's glass doors. "Hurry—the Cougars are leading the Rams in triple overtime. We can still catch the—" He stopped short, entirely forgetting his enthusiasm for the basketball game in his surprise at seeing our longtime friend.

"Well, hullo, Doc," he grinned, reaching out his hand.

"How's it goin'?" Ben answered, clasping my husband's hand heartily. "So they're beating the Rams, are they?"

"Yeah, it's a close fight. Colorado State hung onto a two-point lead most of the fourth quarter," Darren explained. "But BYU will pull it off, of course," he razzed, knowing our friend was a long-time CSU fan.

"Close ones make the best games," Ben grinned.

They went on laughing lightheartedly about a rivalry which, at that moment, didn't matter at all to me. There was one answer I wanted, one thing I'd been eager to ask but didn't know how.

As a physician and as a bishop Ben was obviously very familiar with the problems of abuse. Was it common for mothers to react the way mine had? Why? I'd drawn my own conclusions long ago, but I wanted very much to hear what he'd say.

/ / / 6 / / /

Finally, I could stand it no longer. Ben was telling Darren that he knew Doug Larsen, the Littleton boy who'd made it big with the Colorado State basketball team. I waited only for enough of a pause to be polite.

"Darren," I jumped in. "Did you know Ben is thinking of writing a book?"

"About Doug Larsen?"

"No," I said, swatting him playfully, but my voice was serious. "No, he wants to write something that will help adult survivors of abuse—particularly sexual abuse."

Darren's teasing stopped instantly. A surprised look crossed his face before he smiled. "What a worthwhile project, Ben," he said. Then he added carefully, "And a very much-needed one."

"Yes," Ben answered. "A lot of secular books have been written, but there's a need for more gospel light to be shed on this problem."

"What would you say to LDS people that's different from what therapists say in general?" Darren asked, the Cougars and Rams entirely forgotten.

"Many things are unique about an LDS situation," Ben began, leaning back against the wall and placing the scriptures and organizer he'd been holding on a table nearby. "But one of the most obvious and significant things is the problem of trying to

43

cope if the perpetrator is a priesthood holder. Just think what that can do to someone's testimony."

You're not kidding! I thought. I've always felt that unworthy, insincere priesthood holders who masquerade as good guys must be the worst possible hypocrites. And the sin Christ abhorred most was hypocrisy.

"Surely everyone knows the Church doesn't condone abuse of any kind," Darren said. I could tell he was being cautious: he didn't know how much I'd told Ben about myself. Yet he was as curious about the book as I was. "In general conference President Hinckley read from a letter he'd received, asking him to 'remind the brethren that the physical and verbal abuse of women is INEXCUSABLE, NEVER ACCEPTABLE, . . . especially and particularly despicable if the abuser is a priesthood holder.' "[1]

"Right," Ben said. "But the problem with abuse is that it's almost always a hidden thing. There are times when everyone on the outside thinks the perpetrator is especially nice."

I knew that was true. I remembered when religion first entered my life because with it came the absolutely shocking realization that people who met my dad liked him. People really liked him!

/ / / / /

Right across the street from our house was the library. But there was something far more important about that old adobe building than the books and records inside. What mattered were the lawns.

All the kids in the neighborhood played on those lawns. The grass was thick in the summer, and the sprinklers were wonderfully cool. The palm and date trees posed a climbing challenge, and the orange trees had the sweetest scent and coolest shade. During the rainy season, the library's parking lot was an ocean of puddles, waiting for stick ships and splashing sea monsters and muddy dams. And best of all, the head librarian was a friendly lady, the classic cookie-baking grandma, who didn't mind our happy noise as long as it stayed outside.

One day during the summer I turned ten, Maria's best friend, Angel, called to say that the sprinklers were going. All the kids were putting on their swimsuits and meeting at the library. Would we like to come?

Of course! Mom gave permission, and we excitedly got out our brand-new suits. We had recently been to the store, and I had chosen a great-looking bikini. I'd never had a bikini before, but Maria liked it so much we decided to be "twinners." She'd gotten one exactly like mine.

"Everyone's going to love our new suits," she giggled.

"They'll positively drool," I grinned as I tied back my hair.

Mom met us in the front room. "Here you go, girls," she said, holding out two old towels. "Don't lose them."

"We won't!" I hollered over my shoulder as we ran out the door.

Searing desert sun blazed down on us, and the wet splashy grass beckoned. All the boys and girls from around the neighborhood were running, laughing, happily screaming. We played several variations of tag, making up the rules as we went. Pretty soon I saw Maria and Angel slip over to the warm sidewalk to take a break. They lay down side by side, heads together.

Suddenly I heard Maria crying. Angel was leaving, and a bunch of other girls were trailing behind her. I ran to Maria.

"It's all your fault!" she growled. "Everybody hates me now."

"What'd I do?"

"You picked out this suit," she screamed in my face and pointed at her bikini. "You told me it was the 'in' thing!"

"It is," I answered, shocked. "The lady at the store said so."

Maria wasn't yelling any more. She just flopped back down on the sidewalk and buried her face in her towel. What a dumb thing to make my sister cry about! Angel was so rude. I began to seethe inwardly. Sometimes, Angel appeared to get pleasure from hurting other people's feelings. This time, I decided, she wasn't going to hurt my sister and get away so easily.

I ran as fast as I could down the sidewalk. In my mind, I rehearsed just what I would say. I would be sure to use a cussword or two; that would scare her a little.

"Wait up!" I hollered.

Angel did.

What a dummy! I chortled inwardly.

"Where the heck do you get off hurting my sister's feelings like that?" I yelled as I caught up with her. "Who do you think you are?"

Angel looked up at me with stubborn eyes. Her voice came right back, quick and sharp. "I'm a baptized Mormon, and we don't wear bad things like that." She gestured at my swimsuit. "We're going to heaven, and you're not."

"Am too!" I shouted.

"You can't! You haven't been baptized." Angel's face was smug as she spun away on her heel and went off with her friends.

I turned around slowly, my bare feet slapping loudly against the cement as I walked back to Maria. The anger I'd been feeling had suddenly melted into bewilderment. What on earth was she talking about?

When I put my hand on Maria's shoulder, she stood up. We walked home wordlessly. Why would our friends say such things?

Later that afternoon Maria asked Mom, "What is baptized?"

Mom sat down with us and answered our question the best she could. But I wasn't satisfied. Everything she said led to another question. And I guessed that our questions were too hard for Mom because she stopped right in the middle of one and went into her bedroom. When she came back, she handed me a tiny book. It was covered with white leather, and in small gold letters across the top were the words *New Testament*.

"You girls read this, and you'll find the answers," she said.

I tried hard to read that book. Long after Maria gave up, I was still trying. In fact, I started over several times during the next few weeks. But the words were so funny and strange that I wasn't sure what I'd read from one paragraph to the next.

The little white book frustrated me until I finally gave it back to my mother. "That's the weirdest thing I've ever seen," I said, slipping it onto the counter beside her. I was at the top of my class in reading, but I'd never seen anything as strange as this. "What crazy fool wrote it, anyway?"

Mom was great. She explained that the people who knew Jesus and talked with Him wrote down the things He said and did. That was a long time ago, so the words were old-fashioned.

"How about if I take you and Maria to the church where I went when I was a little girl? I haven't been to mass or gone to confession in nearly thirty years," she mused, mostly to herself. Then, turning back to me, she added, "But you might find some answers there."

So, bright and early Sunday morning, Maria and I put on our best dresses. Mama did our hair extra pretty, spraying some of her very own perfume on us. Then, like every other time we were about to go anywhere, she sat us down to rehearse our manners.

"When we get to the church, follow closely behind me," she instructed firmly. "Do exactly what I do. Don't ever talk above your softest whisper. It isn't proper to speak in church, and it makes the little old ladies very upset." Mom's eyes told us that it was important to do everything exactly right, so we took her instructions seriously.

This was exciting! I'd never been in a church before. But I was a little nervous, too. What if I goofed up?

Anticipation tickled my insides as we filed out the back door and went across to the far stall in the garage, where the car Mom was allowed to drive was parked. She hadn't been driving very long. Although we'd always had two cars in the driveway, she didn't use them much.

"Now be sure there isn't any dirt on your shoes," Mama said. "Daddy has a buyer who wants to look at the car this afternoon."

Daddy liked to buy cars, and he liked to sell them, too. He babied his cars so much that when he sold them, he always made money. This Ford Bronco had lots of rules, and not only for passengers. Now that Mom had a license, she could never go anywhere without first hearing the rules on driving, too.

Before long, Mom pulled up in front of a small stucco

church right in the middle of town. At the front was a pair of giant, wooden doors that were rounded at the top, and there were bells ringing in the tower. We parked and walked quickly into the cool, spicy-smelling dimness. Just inside the heavy doors we found a small entryway with a tiny desk and hooks for hanging coats. Mom signed all our names in a fancy book, and when she straightened up, I took an eager step forward. We were finally going in!

"Wait a second," she whispered, catching at my arm. She pulled three lacy hankies from her purse. "Put these on your heads carefully. You must keep your head covered while you're inside the sanctuary."

Maria and I quickly did as we were told.

"Now," she said, "you're ready for follow-the-leader."

My eyes raced a hundred miles an hour as we stepped through the second doors into the big room. My breath caught at the beauty—this was prettier than I'd ever imagined.

Mom yanked me by the hand. "You've *got* to do as I do," she whispered in my ear.

Mom moved her hand in a sort of circular motion from her head to her shoulders and then curtsied, so Maria and I bobbed up and down, too. Then Mom began walking up the aisle. I wished she would slow down for just one second. I wanted to look around. But she walked forward steadily and then turned sideways into one of the pews. There was a stool pushed under the bench in front of us, and she pulled it out for herself, so we did the same with the one closest to us. Mom knelt down and tugged at our dresses, signaling for us to follow. She pulled a round string of beads from her purse, and Maria immediately asked, "O-o-oh, Mama! Where'd you get that pretty necklace?"

"Sh-h-h-h!" Mama hushed. "It's my rosary. Now, tell the Heavenly Father 'thank you' for letting you come and whatever else you want to thank Him for. Then sit down on the bench—quietly."

I said my thank yous at record speed before scooting up on my seat to look around. On both sides of the sanctuary were tall, colored windows with sunlight streaming through them.

The pretty glass formed bright pictures of men in long robes, and there were words printed below each window, but I was too far away to read them. Ahead of us was a platform with more pews and what Mom called an altar topped by tall, thin candles. On each side of the platform was a pulpit. A lady came in from a door behind one of the pulpits, walked to the organ, and began playing softly. Behind the altar was a giant picture window of Mary holding the baby Jesus, surrounded by tiny blue flowers and streaming rays of gold.

Mom leaned over and whispered, "The windows are beautiful, aren't they, Liz?"

I nodded.

"They're stained glass," she added. "Each little piece was cut by hand." Then she suddenly whispered, "Shhhhh! Get ready—it's time to start follow-the-leader again."

I couldn't believe my eyes. In through the back door came a bunch of boys singing and wearing long white robes that looked like dresses. Behind them was a man in a fancier robe of white and black, with a satin muffler hanging around his neck.

When we sang we stood up, when we prayed we knelt down, and in between we sat and listened. I did my best to stick with the group in standing and kneeling and sitting, but I didn't do such a good job of understanding what the man in the robe was saying. There were too many pretty things to look at.

"It's time for communion," Mama whispered. "You haven't been baptized, so fold your hands this way."

When she saw we were ready, she walked forward to the altar. She ate a piece of cracker and drank some red stuff. The man in the robe drew a cross over my head and Maria's with his thumb. Then he said something—I couldn't understand what—and we were off to Sunday School.

My teacher was real pretty and very nice. She told us a flannelboard story about Jesus feeding a big crowd of people, and she let us color. Maria thought it was fun, too.

After that, Mom came and took us to another room where everyone was eating donuts and drinking coffee. She sat us down with a napkin on our laps and sugary, jelly-filled donuts in our hands. "Wait right here for a minute," she said. "I'm going to go talk to Father Demas." She went over to the man who had been wearing the robe earlier, and then he walked with her toward us.

"Hello, girls. Your mother says you want to be baptized."

I nodded my head and swallowed the bite that was in my mouth. "Yes, sir."

Maria gulped and nodded her head, too.

"Good," the father said, smiling at our mother. "We'll see you Wednesday."

Wow! I thought. *That was easy. Now we'll be baptized. Angel can't ever say Maria and I aren't going to heaven again.*

Wednesday came quickly, and Mom had made some special arrangements. A couple she knew from her job at the school cafeteria met us in the entryway. They were going to be our godparents. Daddy came, too. He was smiling and shaking hands with everybody. Mom's friend was interested in buying Daddy's car, so they were busy talking from the start.

After we sat down, the father stood behind one of the pulpits. He had a pitcher of water that he said a prayer over. Then he asked me to join him, so I walked up the aisle with the ruffles on my best dress swishing around my legs and my shoes quietly thumping against the red, red carpet.

The father took the pitcher and poured it into a little sink beside the pulpit. Then he dipped his fingers in the holy water and sprinkled some of it on my head. "I baptize you in the name of the Father, the Son, and the Holy Ghost."

After that, he called Maria forward and did exactly the same thing to her. "Elizabeth and Maria," the father said, "you are clean and pure now. All your sins have been washed away through the blood of Christ Jesus."

That was all. Now we were baptized, and we were every bit as good as anyone else. Funny, though, I didn't really feel any different.

NOTE

1. Gordon B. Hinckley, "Our Solemn Responsibilities," *Ensign,* Nov. 1991, p. 50.

/ / / 7 / / /

wasted no time telling Angel and the others that Maria and I had been baptized. Not only that, but I'd already memorized some prayers and songs. I even knew that Father Demas's colored mufflers had special meanings, such as green for Easter. Surely our friends would be nicer to us now.

"You got sprinkled?" Angel and her friends snickered. "That doesn't mean a thing."

"Huh?"

"Well," she added snidely, "*your* baptism didn't count. That man did it wrong. It doesn't mean anything."

Maria and I were confused, but we weren't brave enough to ask Mommy any more about it. Daddy had started going to a brick church two blocks down the street (where he'd gone as a boy), and Mommy was taking us to the little stucco church with the bells. They'd been having a lot of arguments about who was right and what was true. There was a lot of yelling going on at our house.

And that was the thing that confused me the most. I was seeing a new side of Daddy since he had started going to church. We'd been living here for two years, but none of these people had ever come to visit. Now the whole neighborhood seemed to like him, and two men had even been coming over every month to see him.

Couldn't any of these people tell how awful he really was? But then again, how could they? He was so nice to them; he smiled and laughed a lot. But I knew, just as when we'd moved into our new house and when he'd adopted us, that nothing about our family had really changed.

Take report card time, for example. No matter how hard Maria and I tried, we were never once able to make that day a good one.

Daddy expected perfection. He told us so lots of times. He said there was absolutely no way he was going to let us make the same mistakes he did. He had quit school when he was a teenager and then he'd gone back to finish years later. Why would I want to do that? I remembered his finishing too well.

It hadn't been long after he and Mama had gone away to Nevada. A couple of nights a week, for a very long time, we drove with Daddy to the community college. He went inside while Mom and Maria and I sat in the car or on the grass for hours, waiting until he came out again. Mama read us stories, and we sang songs with the radio. I still don't know why we had to go with him, but I remember that when he got his high school diploma, he didn't take us along.

So why would he think that because he had to finish school as an adult, we'd want to do it, too? My grades were always A's and B's. Maria had a lot harder time; she didn't seem to be able to remember anything for very long. But her teachers hadn't been holding her back, and she promised she would never drop out.

/ / / / /

One night during parent-teacher conferences, Mommy and Daddy saw the report cards before we did. I wished they would get home. The knot in my stomach was killing me, and Maria had been in the bathroom throwing up. She knew her grades weren't going to be good, and I could tell it, too, just by looking at her. Her face was pale, and her dark eyes frowned with a frightened look.

When the car pulled into the driveway and the door slammed, Maria jumped. Slamming doors were not a good sign.

Before Mama and Daddy even came in, we went into the front room and sat down quietly on the sofa.

Report card day was one of the few times we ever got to go in the front room because it was a place for company. The entire room had been remodeled and carefully decorated in a southwestern style. Visitors always commented on the authentic Navajo blankets, earthen pottery, handwoven baskets, sand paintings, and the extra-big God's-eye hanging above our step-down fireplace.

Daddy came in and found us waiting. I'm the oldest, so I got interrogated first. "You have two B's on your report card this time, Elizabeth." His voice was stern and his gray eyes flashed.

I knew better than to say anything besides "Yes, sir."

"Your cousin Holly always gets straight A's!" he yelled.

Just once I'd like proof! I thought, but I bit my tongue.

"And here, under 'teacher's comments,' there's a section to evaluate if you use your time wisely. Mrs. Goebel has written: 'Usually, but not always.' " He paused just long enough to take a breath. "One week in your room! Time is valuable; stop wasting it, Elizabeth Lynn Hughes."

I knew I was slow once in a while with my work. Sometimes I daydreamed, but whenever I was concentrating I could always do a real good job. Didn't daydreams happen to everyone? They were sure a lot better than nightmares—and I had my share of those, too.

Daddy was still reading aloud from the "teacher's comments" section: "She's a wonderful student, a hard worker. If she could learn to keep her mouth shut, she'd be perfect."

Keep her mouth shut? Mrs. Goebel never said anything like that to me. I enjoyed visiting with my friends, but I had never gotten in trouble for talking too much. I'd never been disciplined in class—I'd have died of embarrassment first. But every time there was a parent-teacher conference, Daddy said that I opened my big mouth too much. I wished I could see that report card—I had a feeling he was lying.

"If you don't learn to keep your mouth shut, I'm going to cut out your tongue!" Daddy yelled. "Two weeks in your room for that, and if you make a peep, I'll add another."

Next came the hard part: Maria's review. If only I could leave; I hated watching this. Daddy always started by asking her why she got this C or that D. Maria always answered, "I don't know."

I sat there wishing Maria would come up with some kind of new response besides "I don't know." Those words really ticked Daddy off bad. Years later I learned that Maria answered that way because it was the truth. She had ADD, attention deficit disorder. But no one understood ADD when she was little. Daddy seemed convinced she was stupid and lazy.

The third time she said "I don't know," Daddy punched her squarely in the mouth with his closed fist. "Well," he drawled coolly, "I don't know why I just did that, either."

Before Daddy finished, Maria had been punched several more times. Her face was already swelling around the nose and eyes. I couldn't keep from crying, and the tears rushed down my cheeks. I felt responsible somehow. We'd worked together on her homework—we'd worked hard. I didn't know what had gone wrong.

"Get out of my sight!" Daddy raged. "You two make me sick. I'm tired of you being an embarrassment to this family!"

I grabbed Maria, and we ran to our room. We got undressed and crawled into bed without even turning on a light. I could hear her crying in the silence, choking on the sobs, trying not to make a sound Daddy might hear. After the television had been turned on in the front room, I scooted to her side of the bed and curled my arms around her shoulders.

Neither of us could go to sleep for a long time. Maria was in a lot of pain. Inside, I was, too. Tomorrow began the "groundation period." Standing and staring at a wall for two weeks was going to be very hard for me. But poor Maria! She would have to stand in her corner until midterms, and then she might get to come out only if her progress reports were extra good.

Whether we slept or not, morning always came. Maria's face

was purplish and swollen. "Wear this yellow dress," I told her. "It doesn't show your face as much."

Maria just looked at me. How can your dress hide your face?

On the way to school, we made a plan to try out at dinnertime. And that evening, when chores were finished and everyone was at the table, things started off like normal.

Daddy was working on Maria between bites. Mealtimes had become very difficult. How could she eat when she was scared stiff trying to remember her times tables? I knew Maria couldn't multiply when the room was so quiet and when she couldn't use her fingers.

"Nine times seven is sixty-three, you dumb retard!" Daddy yelled.

Maria is never going to remember that one, I thought. I could see she was so frightened her mind had gone blank.

But I just kept eating as fast as I could without breaking any dinnertime rules. If I didn't clean my plate, Daddy would get suspicious. That might ruin our plan, so I kept shoveling the mashed potatoes in as fast as I could. Suddenly I heard a smack followed by a clink.

Daddy had thrown his fork at Maria. "Stop fidgeting!" he shouted.

I quickly shoved the last piece of pork chop into my mouth, wiped my face with my napkin, and put my hands in my lap.

"Four times six," Daddy said.

With my hands down where only Maria could see them, I held up two fingers, then closed my fist, then four fingers.

"Twenty-four," Maria answered, but she didn't lift her head to look at him. I didn't blame her for not wanting to look at Daddy, but I wished she'd look up a little, at least as far as her plate, so he wouldn't figure us out.

When Daddy was through eating, he pushed away from the table and spoke smugly. "Let's see how many you can forget by tomorrow night."

As soon as he was gone, Mom took a load of dishes to the sink.

"We did it!" I whispered, smiling at Maria.

My sister looked back at me with eyes full of hate.

"What's wrong?"

"You." Maria tried to force down the last of her food so she wouldn't get into even more trouble. "You think you're so smart."

I didn't understand, but it was better having Maria cross with me than having Daddy mad every second at the dinner table. So I kept on helping her for several months.

One day I could stand the hypocrisy no longer. Though I didn't know that big word, I had a working knowledge of what being two-faced meant. Some nights Daddy put on a grin and headed out to church. They'd made him a deacon in the church down the road, and it seemed to me that he put one face on when he went out the door, but he took it off and put on his old face again when he came back.

He was gone one evening, doing something with his friends at church, and my mother was quietly sitting by the TV, mending.

"Mom?" I began snuggling up next to her. "Why is Daddy so different when other people are around? Why do people like him? Can't they see what he's really like?"

My mother was very intent on her sewing. She had a puzzled look on her face, but she didn't register much emotion. "Your daddy is a very outgoing person," she answered slowly. "He . . . he always has been." She cut a new piece of thread, licked the end, and squinted as she struggled to push it through the eye of the needle. "He has lots of friends. He's fun to be around. People just . . . like him."

Her answer was so matter-of-fact that I was amazed. Maybe I didn't know this guy at all.

Right then, Daddy came in the front door. I took one look. No, I knew him. I knew him too well.

"Did you pick up the litter in the yard?" he snarled angrily, hanging his jacket in the closet.

"Yes," I replied. "I did."

I felt as if Daddy were shooting daggers at me, millions of them, racing, screaming, piercing the air. "Liar!" he growled. "I just checked, and there's a ketchup squeezie lying right in the middle of our front sidewalk."

"But I did pick them up. It was the first job I did after school. Wasn't it, Mom?" I asked, turning around. Mom had put away her sewing and gone downstairs to the laundry room.

"Liar." The word hissed out of his mouth again.

It wasn't a new word. I was so sick of being called a liar that I thought I might explode. "I . . . picked . . . up . . . the papers . . . three . . . or four . . . hours . . . ago." I bit the words out slowly, making each one clear, even though they were coming through my teeth.

"You picked up the papers?" he asked again, sarcastically.

"Yes." There was a time when I would have immediately said I hadn't done that job yet and then run and done it again. But as of this minute, those days were past. From now on, I vowed, once I'd done a job, I'd done it. I was not going to keep repeating my work just to please this monster.

"There is a ketchup packet in the middle of the sidewalk, right?" he asked.

"I guess so," I answered carefully, not wanting to commit myself to anything but the fact that I'd done that job already.

Then Daddy drew the most irrational conclusion I'd ever heard in my life. "If there is anything on the sidewalk, then the trash in our yard hasn't been picked up yet today."

"But . . . but people walking by—"

"No *buts!* If you'd picked up the trash, it wouldn't be there," he shouted. "Now *go* pick it up." He flung the door open for me to walk out. As I stepped past him, Daddy hissed softly, "You're grounded again for lying. Maybe a month will teach you honesty." He slammed the door behind me.

I plodded down the steps and then down our front walk to the sidewalk that paralleled the road. I'd had it. I was so sick of his twisting and arranging everything to make me look bad. I was sick to death of the wall and of chores and of his moodiness. I was sick of name-calling and hatred.

"Fifteen million people, especially kids, walk down this sidewalk every day," I muttered to myself as I bent over and picked up the plastic ketchup container. Didn't Daddy ever stop to think that less than a block away were Joey's Gas and Goodies and Benson's Laundry and around the corner was a Daylight Donut? This ketchup might have been dropped two seconds before he came home. Or a dog might have carried it over from the neighbor's yard. I hated all the inconsiderate slobs who dropped their candy wrappers and donut bags.

Sitting down on the front steps, I squished the red ketchup back and forth inside its plastic package, back and forth, harder and harder. I was full of hate . . . and I hated the hate. There was only one way I could think of to get rid of it, and that was to run away from it. All this hate was too big to fight, too big to overcome.

I stood up and sucked in a very deep breath of hot, dry twilight air. I would run away, but it wouldn't be just yet. He would be watching me now—I couldn't get far enough away— but the right moment would come if I watched carefully.

Putting my hand on the doorknob, I paused and looked back over my shoulder. No, the yard was spotless. There wasn't another piece of trash or a broken stick anywhere. Then I went inside, threw away the crumpled ketchup squeezie, and walked to my wall.

/ / / 8 / / /

I stood with my nose in the corner for a very long time. I imagined I was the size of an ant, climbing up the textured wall the way a mountain climber struggles up a sheer cliff. Then I imagined I was a mouse who had been shrunk by a mad scientist. I was right there on the wall, but no one could see me. Intently, I tried creeping around the grooves as if they were a maze. And just whenever I thought I'd found a way to the top, I always hit a dead end.

"Wake up," Daddy said, thumping me on the back of the head. "Did you hear me?"

"No, sir."

"I said we're leaving. Your mother and I are going to feed the horses. Don't move from this spot, or I'll beat you to a bloody pulp. Do you hear me?"

"Yes, sir," I responded, but my mind silently answered, *You THINK! You'll never beat me again!*

Even before he slammed the back door and stomped down the steps, I'd conjured up a plan. "Maria," I whispered.

The car's engine whined as Daddy backed out of the driveway. "Maria!"

"What?" she answered from her corner, without turning her head.

"I'm going to run away. Do you want to come?"

Maria turned and shrieked in a whisper, "You *what?*"

"You heard me! Are you coming or not?"

She listened a minute to be sure she couldn't hear the car's engine anymore. Then she yelled, "You're nuts!"

"No," I said earnestly. "I'm just tired beyond believing. We've got to try something new. I don't want to spend the rest of my life with my nose in this corner."

"Where are you going?" she asked, and I could see both terror and hope in her eyes.

"I won't tell unless you're with me. I don't want you blabbing to Daddy and Mom."

"Okay . . . I'll come."

I hugged her. Neither of us really wanted to be alone. "Grab your shoes, and we're out of this pit. I'll tell you more as we go."

While we ran down the alley, cut through a dry, abandoned yard, and took another street, I told Maria my plan. "I have this new friend named Andy." Pant, pant, pant. "She's great"—pant—"really tops. . . . And she lives pretty far away." A car turned onto the street, its headlights crashing around the corner. I pulled Maria down, and we crouched next to some cactus and boulder landscaping. Then, as we got back on our feet, I added the real insurance: "Dad doesn't know her, and he doesn't know where she lives."

When we reached the right house, we stopped to catch our breath. Maria's brown eyes were wide in the darkness. "It's okay, Maria," I said. "Her dad sells stuff, so he travels a lot, and her mother's super nice." Maria wasn't convinced. I didn't want her to start crying now. "Andy is great. She has a trampoline in her backyard and a big trunk full of her great-grandmother's dresses that she can play in. You'll love her house." Then, without giving Maria another moment to hesitate, I reached up and rang the bell.

As if she knew how desperately I wanted her to, Andy opened the door. "L-Liz?" she stammered in surprise. "H-H-Hi!"

"Hi, Andy," I said, trying to look as if being out alone after dark was a real natural thing. "This is my sister, Maria."

"Mom," Andy called. "A friend of mine from school and her sister are here. Can they come in?"

"Sure."

"Let's go to your room. We *have* to talk," I whispered to Andy as we hurried in the door. I had to make sure she understood that we weren't running away from the events of today. We were running away from years of this. Since I was four, every day had been filled with fear, and the really big blowups were coming more and more often. Soon people weren't going to believe our bruises had come from doorknobs and cupboard handles. I spoke so quickly, so desperately, that Andy never even had a chance to say a word. Then, realizing how I'd rambled, I stopped short and looked into her eyes.

They were filled with shock. "How can I ask my parents to help you?" she moaned sadly. "I'm not sure they'll believe me."

A wave of desperation washed over me, and I thought I might drown. Maria was crying. "Please, Andy. Oh, please . . . *please* try. We'll leave quickly if your mom says no. We'll find help somewhere else. But we can't go back—he said he'd beat us to a pulp if we left the wall, and he really will."

I think Andy could feel our despair, our hopeless fear. She thought about it for a long time and then drew a deep breath. "Here goes nothin'."

As soon as Andy went out of the room, Maria slid across the bed until she was beside me. "What if her mom calls Daddy?" she whispered.

The thought sent an electric surge of fear racing to my fingers and toes. How could I have been such an idiot? I'd never thought of that. I'd handled everything all wrong. "We'll just have to hope she doesn't," I told Maria, trying to sound optimistic. Andy would have let us play with her things, I knew, but Maria and I just sat on the bed, holding hands.

I noticed that Andy had taped up posters and pictures of friends all over the place. I wondered what I would do if I ever had the chance to make my room the way I wanted it. But I didn't wonder long—unless a miracle happened, that question was pointless.

"You're safe for now," Andy said, walking back into the room with an enormous grin. "My dad gets home from a trip to

Phoenix later tonight, though, and it all depends on what he says."

Maria and I sat and stared at her. Eventually, I tried to pull up a smile from my stomach.

"Come on," Andy said, grinning again. "There's nothing else we can do. Let's have a little fun until we see what happens. Have I ever shown you the opera fan and tiara my great-grand-mother had?"

Like a thirsty man in the desert, we jumped into Andy's mirage of play. We had a marvelous time until the front door clicked shut.

"It's your dad!" Maria breathed.

We listened as Andy's mother greeted him and took him into another room. They closed the door. I strained to hear what they were saying. Maybe we could still run if we had to . . . but we couldn't make out a word they said.

Then Andy's parents came out of the room. They walked right past us into the kitchen without even acknowledging that we were there. "It's okay!" Andy whispered. "Let's go play some more."

I wanted to believe her. I wanted so much to believe her that I followed her back into her room. So did Maria. Soon we were swimming again in the world of imagination.

Suddenly all the walls came crashing down around me. My mouth was full of sawdust. My heart pounded painfully. My face burned. *No!* my whole soul silently screamed. *No! No! No!*

Daddy was standing in the doorway.

He looked taller than he ever had before. His calm, second face beamed down at us. In the voice he saved for other people to hear, he said, "Come on, girls. It's time to go home."

I couldn't feel my feet as I stood up to obey. It felt as if someone else guided my body out of Andy's house and into the car. The ride home was a blur. I was totally detached, with no emotion left, without a grip on what was happening. My body went into the house and up the stairs I had hoped so earnestly never to see again.

Slam! A big foot nailed me from behind. I went sailing down the varnished hallway floor, not stopping until I hit the carpet of my own bedroom. Before I was even sure what had happened, Maria landed on top of me. I could distantly hear her sobbing as my body struggled to get back on its feet.

I looked up. When my eyes met Daddy's, his fist hit my cheek. He must have hit me real hard because the next thing I knew, I was flat on my back again. I thought my head was throbbing, but I wasn't sure of anything.

"Look what you did!" Daddy screamed. "Look! Look, you little creep!"

Somehow, my eyes followed his finger, and I saw a big dent in the wall. Then I found myself facedown on my bed. Maria was next to me. Daddy was spanking her with a wooden hanger, and after a while I began distantly counting the strikes. I knew he would give me more than he gave her because I was older—he always made a point of telling me that.

When Daddy started in on me, my mind told me I was in severe pain: my head was hurt, and my bottom was in agony. But I escaped into the fog as much as I could. Sometimes the fog deserted me, and there was nothing but horrible, red pain. Other times I could run away where it almost seemed the nightmare was happening only to my body, not to me.

I refused to cry out loud. I'd become a stone. It would be better to die than to endure this ever again.

"So you're real tough today, huh?" Daddy shouted, hitting me on the head. "Well, take this!" He jerked off my pants and whaled on my bare skin.

There was no more fog. Lost in fiery, burning, throbbing pain, I screamed. Even then, Daddy kept going for a while before he quit.

Still lying face down with my pants pulled off, I heard him shout as he stomped to the door. "Whatever goes on in this house is our business. *No one* else's. Don't ever open your ugly mouths again—" he glared back at us through the doorway, *"ever!"*

/   /   /   /   /

"As Elizabeth and I were saying earlier," Ben told Darren, "there are certain variables that make a big difference in how lasting the effects of abuse are. Aside from the severity of the abuse itself, the first variable is whether physical violence was involved."

"I can understand that," Darren responded.

"Another factor is the victim's closeness to the abuser. If a child is abused by a neighbor or a baby-sitter the child sees occasionally, the effects aren't as devastating as if the child's own father is the perpetrator."

"Sure," Darren nodded. "It's a lot easier to conclude your neighbor is awful than to tell yourself that your dad is a wicked, evil man."

"Exactly," Ben said. "And that's especially true if 'Dad' seems to be a great guy in other ways." He paused. "Of course, the third variable is the length of the abuse. How long did it go on? How many incidents were there?"

Darren nodded.

"And the final, most significant factor is how the mother responds."

Oh, good, I thought. *Here's the answer to my question about why mothers so often disbelieve.*

"Now, there's a catch," Darren said. "Why in the world wouldn't a mother believe her own child? I mean, this is a child she has known longer and more intimately than anyone else has. Surely she can tell whether her own child is telling the truth."

"She probably can," Ben answered. "But she may not allow herself to believe what she senses to be true. Most of the time, there are two main reasons for her response. First, these women have often been victims themselves. Just this week, I treated a patient in my office who, now that she is in her forties, has finally gotten brave enough to ask her mother why she didn't help. There was no doubt her mother had known what was going on all the time."

"And?" I asked.

"And her mother responded with, 'What's the big deal? That

happened to me when I was small. No one ever took care of me. How was I supposed to take care of you?' "

"In other words," I said, "her trust had been so shattered as a child that protecting someone else or keeping someone else's trust was simply beyond her. Is that what she meant?"

"Yes," Ben answered. "Apparently it never occurred to her that she could make a conscious decision to stop the cycle of abuse. She seems to have accepted it as a part of real life. Either that, or thinking about her daughter's abuse meant she would have to think about her own abuse . . . and that was simply too much for her to handle."

The hall was very quiet. "You said there was another reason why some mothers don't nip the problem in the bud," I prodded.

"Right," Ben said, drawing a deep breath. "Especially in cases of sexual abuse, mothers are afraid to disrupt their family. If a woman believes and accepts what her daughter is saying, then the crime is so heinous she has to take drastic action."

Darren and I nodded.

"Turning her husband over to the authorities is a big thing to do. It may ruin his business—not only his livelihood but that of herself and her children. It may ruin his reputation and tarnish everyone else's. It may ruin his standing in the Church and indirectly affect the entire family's. The ramifications of causing so much turmoil are often too big to think about for a woman whose self-esteem is already hurting. Her mind may tell her she can't support the children. She may begin to count the tender testimonies that could be hurt when she uncovers her husband's deceit. She feels as if she should have kept this from happening. Somehow, she begins to think *she* has failed."

"That's even easier to see within the Church because of our emphasis on family life," I agreed.

"The Church's orientation is good and right," Darren countered. "Encouraging lasting commitment in families doesn't mean we want to perpetuate abuse."

"You and Ben and I know that," I said, somewhat surprised. "But some people have misinterpreted it."

Darren grinned and agreed. "Breaking out of a harmful marriage could feel like a failure, when, in fact, it is the bravest thing some women could ever do."

"But there are times when women read scriptures about forgiveness and love and feel confused," I said. I'd seen that confusion. "It might seem the Christlike thing to give unconditional love and try to patch things up."

"It might seem that way," Ben said emphatically, "but abuse is different from almost any other situation. We're not encouraging wholesale divorce or rampant inquisition. Still, overlooking abuse in the name of forgiveness doesn't help anyone. You have to draw the line somewhere. And no matter what, any kind of sexual abuse is clearly wrong."

Suddenly the hall was silent again. Ben was looking right at me. "I'm not advocating revenge or retribution," he said. "I'm not saying we shouldn't love the perpetrator. The Savior would have us love all God's children." Deep meaning and emotion surged through his words. He'd obviously struggled somewhere, sometime, with forgiveness. "What I am saying is that the best and greatest love would be to get help for that abuser." He took a deep breath. "If only mothers could see."

/ / / 9 / / /

There was a time when thinking about my mother's blindness to the situation frustrated me terribly. Actually, I seethed with anger at her lack of response. She always disappeared whenever conflicts arose. Even if she didn't actually get up and leave the room, she somehow melted away: dropped her head, sank into the sofa, never said a word. Not once did she ever tell Daddy to stop.

Later, Mom sometimes came into Maria's and my room and said she loved us. Often, on the day after a really big thrashing, we'd come home from school to find a double batch of cookies cooling on the counter. We got to eat half, and the rest were saved for Daddy. Mom never said we shouldn't tell Daddy what she'd done. We simply knew. Although her apologies were subtle, we accepted and understood them.

Was she unable to see what was going on? No. If she had been, there would have been no extra "I love yous" and cookies. But our situation had strapped great big blinders on her, and she hadn't torn them off.

The violence ate at her, too. You can't live in the middle of hate and anger and perversion without having the tension rub off on you. She was near the breaking point—even behind her blinders—and sometimes it showed.

/ / / / /

One afternoon I was in trouble for not completing my morning

68

chores before school. The infraction really wasn't too great: I simply hadn't vacuumed my bedroom. My plan was to come straight home from school and do it before Daddy got off work.

Maria and I called Mom's vacuum The Squid. Mom loved her canister vacuum because of all its wonderful attachments, but as Maria put it, The Squid was a royal pain to drag around. It was always grabbing something.

Unfortunately, my good intentions to rendezvous with The Squid came too late. Company had dropped by. Even though it was only Nanny Julie, Mom was embarrassed that our house hadn't been one hundred percent presentable.

When I walked in the door, Mom was plugging in The Squid and crying. "It's about time!" she yelled and thrust the nozzle in my direction.

Like a dummy, I ducked. The Squid decked me. The area just above my eye tore open. Blood gushed everywhere.

Mama called Daddy, who had to leave work half an hour early. Off to the emergency room we went, where I got my first five stitches and heard the biggest lie of my young life. *That's not at all what happened!* I thought. But my situation was bad enough without my piping up about a little issue like the truth.

Daddy yelled all the way home. He said if I had done my work when I was supposed to, nothing would have gone wrong. He went to great effort explaining how I always made life difficult.

Naturally, I was grounded again as soon as we got home. I also received a new chore of vacuuming the entire house every morning before school for two months. Daddy hoped that would teach me to respect how much work goes into paying stupid doctor bills.

The longer Daddy shouted, the more upset he got. He shouted obscenities and shoved me a few times. He even slapped me across my face. I was so tired I didn't care how long the reprimanding went on. I only wanted to go to bed, to be invisible, to stop existing.

Later that evening Mom came into my bedroom, where I

was standing in my corner. She asked how my head felt—did I need anything for a headache?

"Yeah," I said, astonished to discover that I still had enough strength to be angry with her. "Why don't you send Daddy in to slap me around a little more? That ought to make it feel real good."

I thought Mom would be shocked and hurt, but she just snapped right back, "Well, Elizabeth Lynn, if you weren't so stupid, that vacuum wouldn't have hit you in the face. You should've taken it from me when I handed it to you."

"You chucked it," I said smugly, turning so that my swollen eye and bloody bandage were aimed right at her.

"Chucked it? I *handed* it!" She bit her finger and looked down. Then, lowering her voice but unable to control its tone, she went on, "Next time do your work." Walking out the door she muttered, "If you two kids would just do your work, Daddy wouldn't be angry all the time."

Sure, I thought as I watched Mom leave. *All I need to do is figure out how to be perfect. If I were like Jesus, I'd be safe.* I turned my nose back into the corner, fuming sarcastically to myself. *Just name me one person who's accomplished that! For some reason, God made only one perfect person. I wish I'd been that lucky.*

/ / / / /

"You know what I think?" I said suddenly. "No one's perfect." Ben and Darren looked at me curiously. "I mean, when we're children, either we think our parents are perfect or we feel they ought to be. But the truth is, we're all like pieces of marble. I had a friend once who was a sculptor. She taught me a lot of things about stone that have helped me better understand people."

I'd never told Darren about the ideas I'd had after visiting Becky's studio. But the truth is, while you are overcoming abuse—at least right at first—it pretty much monopolizes your thoughts. Until I really put it to rest, just about everything that crossed my mind tied into my past one way or another.

I smiled at Darren as I went on. "Marble is a supremely beautiful but flawed stone. Inside most pieces you can find a dark flaw—some bigger than others. Some even contain black pits of sand. Often, those sand pits are hidden in such a way that no one, or almost no one, knows they're there. Sometimes the marble has been carefully polished and the sand pit is buried in the middle where it can't be seen, but the flaw is still there."

Darren's eyes seemed to be trying to see through me. "Are you saying all people are innately evil?"

"No, I just mean we're all human, all imperfect," I clarified. "Family members shape one another constantly. They have such close and interdependent relationships that their influences mold one another all the time. In a sense they sculpt each other."

"But—" Darren began.

"Oh, I know each of us has the most control over his or her own life—or if we don't, we need to take it. The Lord shapes us constantly, too, and you can't underestimate His influence. But after that, our family relationships make the most difference."

Ben had been silently listening. Now he mirrored my words back to me. "So you're saying that since we are like sculptors, we have a much closer and more influential relationship with family members than anyone else. Our close contact also makes us more aware of each other's flaws than anyone else could be."

"Yes! And sometimes we even polish one another to hide them."

/ / / / /

For a long time I resented my family's sand pits. Maria and I had defects, I knew. Daddy had mapped them out well for us. And I was sure my mother's weaknesses had left her spineless. But most of all, I hated the big, hideous, black sand pit that filled the hollow heart of my daddy.

There were times when I had concluded that there was no love in him and that he'd sucked it all out of my mother, too. When he wasn't around, she was warm and loving, but when he was, he demanded all her attention.

The night my face was stitched up was one of those times I concluded there was no love in our home—and probably not in the whole world, either. After Mom left the room muttering, I leaned the side of my head against the wall and closed my eyes against its painful throbbing.

I hated her. Inwardly, I blamed her for marrying Daddy and letting such a monster into our home to chew up our lives. I loathed her inability to do anything about the situation.

And in that moment, I hated God, too. Maybe even more than anyone else. Mama couldn't help herself. She never claimed to be all-knowing and all-powerful. But God did. He'd made me and put me in this awful place with these awful people. Some friend! He must not have thought much of me, and I decided I didn't think much of Him or all that wonderful love Father Demas was always talking about. I hadn't seen any of it.

One father in heaven and one on earth. Didn't people always say, "like father, like son"? If my father was a monster, then God must be infinitely worse—a monster like Daddy but multiplied more times than I could think of. This reasoning told me that God was powerful, controlling, stern, strict, and terrifying. Well, I wasn't going to give my love or trust to anyone who called himself father.

I leaned there, with my head throbbing and my stomach tied in knots. Hot tears slid between my closed eyelids and down my cheeks. Hate. *Hate. HATE!*

Then, deep inside me something whispered, *Elizabeth, you know that's not true. Is that really what you want to believe?*

I ignored the feeling—I even tried hating it—but finally I answered that soundless inner voice. My thoughts said, *Oh yes it is true. I hate them, and I hate God most of all. Everyone's a jerk!*

Mentally saying those words felt good. They made the anger rush through me again, vindicating my hatred and releasing me from feeling that I had to try anymore.

But the whisper was still there, inside me, and I knew it was right. I didn't admit it that night, but eventually, I knew, I would listen to it again. When I did, it never let me down. In reality, that inner voice was my best friend.

/ / / / /

Darren slid his arm around my waist. When I raised my eyes, I saw Ben was gazing kindly at me.

"I'm speaking from experience," I said, and my voice wavered.

"I know," he answered softly.

"My childhood was like a roller coaster—up and down, up and down. I always kept grasping at hope, looking for it even when it was nowhere to be found." Darren and Ben didn't answer as the force of my emotion surged through the hall. But their silence wasn't awkward. Rather, they recognized the reality of my long-ago pain, and they knew better than to insinuate that a pat on the back or a cheerful comment could erase it as if it had never been.

Darren pulled out his handkerchief, and I dabbed at my eyes. After a moment or two Ben picked up his scriptures and organizer from the table where he'd set them and asked, "Want to sit down?"

He fitted a key into the lock, twisted it, and swung his office door open. "I would," he said, answering his own question and extending his hand as an invitation to enter. "It would do me good to hear your story, especially since this subject is already so heavily on my mind." He paused. "But if you don't want to talk about it, Liz, that's okay."

I looked up at Darren and then answered by walking in and taking a seat. Darren was right behind me.

Ben pulled his chair from behind his desk and pushed it over close to us. He wasn't beaming any big smiles toward me, but the creases were back at the corners of his eyes.

"I can talk." I answered. "Maybe it will help you if you ever do write that book you're thinking about."

"No doubt," Ben smiled. "I'd especially like to know how you dealt with the hurt. I realize, now, that you've dealt with terrible pain and yet . . . well, until tonight I hadn't seen any signs of it."

"I've made my peace," I responded.

I don't feel that agony anymore, in the sense of carrying it around all the time. But when I open up those emotions and allow myself to remember the crushing hurt that filled those years, well . . . it was very real.

I used to say to myself, *If only we could be perfect.* My ten-year-old eyes couldn't understand that everyone else has sand pits, too. They may not be hideous black ones, but everyone has troubles and weaknesses.

I wished I were perfect, and I wished my family were, too. As I grew older, I often retreated to a mental fairyland where everyone was perfect and things were wonderful. When reality drew me out and shattered my ability to pretend, my outlook became very cynical. Then everyone had those black, abusive pits. The whole world had them and hid them. If it weren't so, someone would surely be doing something about it. Someone would care.

Now I realize that neither the perfect fairy-tale world nor the totally demonic one is realistic. But I couldn't find a niche I could hold onto in between. Years passed as I rode the roller coaster between the two extremes.

During the year I was eleven, the roller coaster climbed upward. Things were unbelievably good—almost frighteningly good—and I actually began to believe my fairy-tale world was coming true.

/ / / 10 / / /

Only a couple of days after I'd battled The Squid, Daddy put on his second face and his new Scout uniform and went down the street for a Young Men's Mutual meeting.

"All my friends' big brothers really like Daddy," Maria commented softly, staring at him through the window as he hurried down the steps and walked briskly away.

"Name one."

"Oh, Candi's and Jeannie's brothers. Angel's, too."

I made a repulsive face to show what I thought of their opinion.

"Whitney's brother told me he's real funny. Her mom said you can tell when someone's really meant for their calling—he said that means a church job—because they enjoy every minute of the work."

Whitney's mom had a point there. Daddy loved doing the kinds of projects the Scouts were involved in: hiking, fishing, camping, mechanical repairs. More and more often it seemed that whenever he came home from a church meeting, a great big grin was spread across his face. He whistled lots of tunes we'd never heard, and he began giving a prayer before dinner sometimes. As much as I hated admitting it, this new smiling Daddy was a very likable person.

One day at dinner, Daddy kissed Mama as he sat down and thanked her for making such a nice meal. Then, about halfway into the mashed potatoes, he asked, "Why don't you all come to sacrament meeting with me this Sunday?"

Maria dropped her fork, and her eyes lit up like stars. "Will Angel and Whitney be there?" she chirped.

"Yes, Gilly-monster. You three will all be in the same Primary class."

Primary, Mutual, sacrament meeting—his church sure had a lot of weird words. "Mom, are you going, too?" I asked.

Mom didn't look up from her plate. Her voice was soft and almost hesitant as she answered, "If you girls would like to go, I'll go, too."

Maria was excitedly trying to capture her peas with her fork. She was obviously delighted about getting increased social time.

A few kids from my school went to that church. The boy, Don, hadn't impressed me very much, and the other two were girls. One was Teri, a new kid in our neighborhood. I felt a little sorry for her. Teri's dresses were hand-me-downs, and she had only two. I supposed having eleven brothers and sisters explained some of her troubles. She had a last name the other kids could twist and use to make fun of her, too. But the other girl, Sandy, was really nice and popular as well. Maybe Maria wasn't the only one who could get a little social time out of this.

"We're in the Third Ward," Daddy said proudly. "Our chapel was one of the first ones built in this area."

Mom made a funny face that sort of said, "So what?"

"You mean *your* church," I corrected. "We got baptized into the Catholic Church, so it can't be *our* church."

Daddy smiled and flatly ignored my observation. And, like always, he got his way. Sunday afternoon we all got dressed up and went to his church.

As we entered the glass doors, we found ourselves in a foyer packed with chattering people. There were the Bensons who lived right next door and owned the corner laundry. I also saw the Farfans, who lived on the other side of us, the Rawsons, the Guzmans, the Smarts, Don's parents and sister, Teri's big family, and lots of Maria's friends. I had to work hard to stick with Mama, who was following Daddy through some open doors.

The chapel wasn't anything like our sanctuary downtown. It was lit by electric lights rather than candles. And there weren't any fancy glass windows or prayer stools. I decided it was humble and simple but pretty in its own way. The padded benches were great.

And the meeting was about as different from our church as the building itself was. Babies had been brought right into the chapel, and they got away with crying out and making noises. Even some big kids were whispering. I thought the little old ladies would be furious, but they all seemed to be smiling as if they didn't care.

I kept waiting for when we'd have to stand to sing and kneel to pray, but it never happened. Although they called it the sacrament, the communion prayers at Daddy's church seemed pretty much like the ones I knew. No one wore robes, though, and they forgot to sing "O Holy." Some boys passed bread and water around to everyone, too, instead of having people come forward.

Daddy pointed out someone he called the bishop and told me that man was the leader, like Father Demas. I kept waiting for this bishop to preach, but he let the other guys do the talking. The main sermon came from a man Daddy called the "high councilman." He told one story I thought was especially interesting. He said it came from the Book of Mormon, so I decided I'd try to check that one out at the library during the next week. The last Indian story I'd read had been about Squanto, and I was curious to know more about Native Americans.

When the meeting ended, we didn't go to Sunday School class. That had been in the morning, Daddy explained. Maria began to pout, and I couldn't hide my disappointment, either. Sunday School was the biggest reason we'd come.

But just then a lady walked over and shook our hands. She smiled as she asked us our names and invited us to Primary. It would be Wednesday afternoon, after school, if we could wait that long.

Then Daddy took my hand and led us into a really pretty room. There were padded folding chairs and a lacy cloth on the table at the front. A nice painting of a mother and baby gazed at us from one wall, a shiny upright piano was pushed into the corner, and a pretty cross-stitch picture hung by the door. "This is the Relief Society room," Daddy said, squeezing my hand and smiling at Mom. He reached out and gently straightened Maria's curls. "We'll just wait a minute for the bishop and his counselors to get here. I'm going to be ordained a priest today."

I had no idea what he was talking about, but I liked this new side of my daddy. Pretty soon some men came in and stood around him in a circle with their hands on his head. I was so glad it was him and not me! I'd always been claustrophobic, and the packed foyer had made my stomach churn. There was no way I could have sat and listened to a prayer with all those men smothering me, but Daddy seemed to be enjoying every word.

They gave the longest prayer I'd ever heard but, it said exactly the things I thought Daddy needed. When they blessed him to choose the right, I mentally whispered, *That means no lies!* They blessed him to have a sharp mind, and I added my own request that his logic would improve on trash pickup in our yard. They blessed him that he would read good books, and I almost stood up to shout, *Yes! Yes! Let's lose the tool chest!* They blessed him to be a good husband, and I knew that meant no yelling at Mom. But when they blessed him to be a good father, all my insides turned over with burning hope. My heart cried, *No more beatings, no more beatings!*

I couldn't believe how right that blessing was. Silently, I prayed, *Please God, make it all come true. Make it be true!*

/ / / / /

"You know," I said to Darren and Ben, "hope is a funny thing. Without it people become brittle and cynical; they lose their ability to see the world clearly or to have joy. But watching your hopes get bashed over and over can be excruciatingly painful. Pretty soon you know you don't want to be hopeless, but you become afraid to hope."

The year I was eleven, I still hadn't lost hope. A little part of me desperately wanted to believe my fairy-tale world would come true. Five more years passed before I became entirely too hurt and uncertain to venture any hope. And until then, my roller coaster was zooming upward to a height from which it would eventually take a dizzying fall.

Ben smiled. His voice was soft but very clear. "Being able to keep your hope alive depends on whom you place it in."

/ / / / /

We celebrated Daddy's being made a priest by eating dinner with some of his friends that night. I didn't care much for the Rawsons, though. They had lived next to us in the trailer court, and they'd been too stuck-up to socialize with us then. But now that Daddy was playing their game, they wanted to get together. No thanks.

Daddy didn't seem to mind at all, though. He was happy about everything, laughing and talking in such a friendly voice. Between his good humor and the blessing those men had given him, I was willing to put up with the Rawson family's changeable hospitality.

Mom was bustling around in the kitchen with Sister Rawson (Daddy told us to call her that), and they were piling the table with a glazed ham, baked potatoes, fruit salad, and lots of other fixings. After we all sat down, Brother Rawson said a blessing on the food. Carrying on with Daddy over one of his jokes, our host began dishing up food for everyone.

Then it happened. As Brother Rawson passed my plate, my fingers slipped, and I dropped the whole thing in my lap. I was mortified! "It's o-o-o-o-ka-a-ay," I stuttered. Not looking up, I tried to make my voice light. "It all landed in my napkin."

That was when I felt his hand on my shoulder. Fear jammed through my limbs like an electrical shock. I knew he was going to slug me. I jerked away.

"Hold still, silly," Daddy said with a laugh, as he picked up my napkin. He dumped my dinner back onto the plate. "Eat it," he said under his breath, right next to my ear. Then he stood up tall, smiling again as he returned to his seat.

Maria giggled and chattered with Heidi Rawson all through dinner, but I could hardly force my mouth open to get the food in. I knew I was in big trouble. *Please, God,* I silently pleaded, *please make those men's blessing come true. At least, please let my beating not be too bad.*

When we went home at last, I kept expecting the harsh words to begin. The longer Daddy waited, the worse I knew it would be. But it never happened.

My shock was so great that I finally went in on my bed and just sat there. I couldn't believe it. *Maybe God really does hear prayers,* I thought.

The events of that day gained more and more significance for me as time went on. Because of the direct correlation I'd seen between prayer and change, a small light began to shine at the end of my life's dark tunnel. Like the tiny voice inside me, this experience with prayer became a beacon pointing me away from cynical hopelessness. There would be times when I was afraid to trust or hope, but I never forgot my first answered prayer.

Over the next few weeks, we continued going to Daddy's church, and I got to know Teri pretty well. She had a cute sense of humor and a thoughtful heart. At first I'd felt sorry for her because she had only one dress and she shared her room with three sisters. But the closer I got to Teri, the better I understood how true envy feels.

Every night when Teri's father came home from work, he hugged his children and talked to them about their day. All eleven of her brothers and sisters actually ran to the door when their dad drove up! Not only that but even though he was dirty and greasy from his job, he'd throw his arms around them and kiss their faces. Then he'd hunt through the house until he found their mom.

Another thing that made Teri's dad so neat was that he always left a few tidbits in his lunch pail. When the children came running to greet him, the ones who didn't get the first hugs got to dig through his leftovers and nibble whatever they could find. The family was poor, and I don't ever remember them finding more than a cookie or a scrap of bread, but the kids gobbled it up like candy because it came from their dad. He must have made a point of leaving treasures in between the empty sandwich bags and napkins on purpose, just for them.

Watching this nightly ritual at Teri's house always embarrassed me. But whenever I was at home and my daddy came in the door, that scene kept reappearing before my eyes. I wished I was brave enough to run to him. I wished he'd hug me.

So it isn't hard to see why I liked being at Teri's house—even if it was embarrassing. But then one day my mom said she didn't like me playing there. From her explanation I gathered that Teri's family was the target of the local grapevine. Everyone accused her parents of neglect, and the gossips even whispered about government social workers investigating the situation. Everyone said they were so concerned about those poor children. But that's all they were: poor. There were eleven children under the age of eighteen in Teri's family, and her mom had decided to stay home to care for them. Their house was cluttered but never dirty. The meals were simple, but they ate them together—happily. Teri's dad worked for the sanitation department, and it's true, he didn't bring home much money. But I never saw him hit anyone.

Mom was worried about the gossip. "Don't go over there so much," she said one evening. "There are lots of other nice girls you know."

"But I like Teri," I told her. "I like her parents." Inside, I was angry about everyone's preoccupation with how much money her dad made. Couldn't they see the double standard? Couldn't anyone see that even though our family never wanted for a single possession, we were crying out for love?

I wished I was brave enough to explain the hypocrisy of it all to Mom. I wanted to make her see how shallow our lives were and how rich Teri's family really was. But my dad was sitting in his chair reading the newspaper, and I kept my mouth shut.

"Well, Liz," Mom said, "just don't spend so much time with her. There are lots of nice girls from fine families in your class at school."

"Aw, Maureen," Daddy spoke from behind his paper. "You worry too much. Let Frecklie-frog play with Teri. After all, their family goes to church every Sunday, so they can't be too bad an influence."

I couldn't believe my ears. Daddy was standing up for me! Perhaps his reasoning wasn't quite the same as mine, but I liked having him on my side of an issue.

Mom snatched up a stack of laundry and went to put it away. In spite of my current joy, I couldn't help but see the bitterness in her face. That look had been there a lot lately. Although she hadn't said it in so many words, I knew Mom was going to Daddy's church in an effort to bring our family together.

They weren't yelling at each other about what was true anymore, but Mom still had obvious misgivings. Her attitude spoke even more loudly than her former arguing had. Daddy seemed happier, Maria and I were certainly happier, but Mom hadn't changed. She'd always pumped the rest of the family up, and now she was lagging behind.

I decided to ignore whatever was troubling Mom. This new personality of Daddy's was much better than anything else I'd ever known. Maybe my prayers *were* being answered. "Excuse me, Daddy," I said. " 'The Waltons' is going to be on TV pretty soon. I've done my homework and my chores. May I watch it?"

"Okay," Daddy said generously, folding his paper and standing up. "Let me check your work."

He found only one thing to complain about, and I did it over quickly, hoping I wouldn't miss the beginning of my show. There was something special about "The Waltons" for me. At the same time Daddy began softening, I had come to love that program. When I watched it, I found myself dreaming of a whole new life-style. In my imagination we all loved each other and would go out of our way to do things for each other. We even prayed together every day.

At bedtime I used to lie very still, squeeze my eyes shut tight, and pretend we were all calling good night to one another. In my mind "Good night, Jim-Bob," "Good night, John-Boy," and "Good night, Mary Ellen," turned into "Good night, Mama. Good night, Daddy. Good night, Maria." But best of all was their imaginary reply: "Good night, Elizabeth."

/ / / 11 / / /

"How would you girls like to be baptized at Dad's church?" Mom asked one day over dinner.

Maria and I sat and stared. She could just as easily have asked us if we'd packed up for a trip to the moon.

Our shock forced a wry grin onto her face, and she repeated the question. "Baptized . . . you know? Daddy's church?" She pointed over her shoulder with her thumb, in the direction of the chapel.

"We can do that?" Maria asked.

"Yes, you can," Daddy answered. "Then you'd be a Mormon, like me."

The grin was gone from Mom's face, but I couldn't read anything in her voice as she went on. "I believe your daddy's church is a good one. I've agreed to be baptized and become a member of it. You girls could be baptized, too." Perhaps I just imagined it, but I thought a little enthusiasm crept into her voice as she added, "We could all do it together."

My sister was entirely for it. She'd never gotten over that swimsuit affair or Angel's claim that sprinkling didn't count. Maria was still trying to be as good as everyone else.

"Yeah, me too," I said. I liked Daddy's church—particularly its improvements on Daddy. "I sure hope they do it right this time, though."

"I promise I will," Daddy said.

84

"*You* will?" I blurted out, noting that he was delighted with my surprise. "How? You're not the bishop."

"No, but I am a priest—remember? Priests can baptize. I'm not an elder yet, so someone else will confirm you, but I can do the baptizing."

The following days were filled with excitement over the white dresses Mom was sewing for us and our curiosity about getting immersed. I noticed Mom wasn't smiling or humming much anymore. She seemed very quiet, and what she did say lacked feeling. Looking back, I'm certain she wasn't doing this because she believed the teachings she'd heard at church. I can't remember her studying any manuals or reading the Book of Mormon. No, Mom was getting baptized as a sacrifice, hoping to pull her family together.

One brilliantly sunny January day we drove to the stake center to be baptized. Our white dresses were spotless and fresh, and the room was packed with all our new friends. After some singing and a talk, Daddy took Mom's hand and helped her down the steps into the font. Then, before I knew it, it was my turn!

Daddy took my hands gently, yet firmly, in his. His touch was kind, and his voice rang out clearly as he spoke the words of the baptismal prayer, beginning with my name: "Elizabeth Lynn Hughes, having been commissioned of Jesus Christ . . ."

There was something so wonderful, so new and different about him, that it would have made the day memorable all by itself. But the greatest moment was yet to come. As soon as Daddy had laid me down in the sparkling clear water, he pulled me gently back toward the surface. As I rose up, the most wonderful feeling I'd ever had in my life descended over me. Something very important had happened. I *knew* it. A power far greater than me was speaking through that little voice inside my heart. And that voice told me with absolute sureness that—independent of Daddy and Mama and whatever reasons I'd had for being here—this was the most right thing I'd ever done.

/ / / / /

Ben's comment about hope repeated itself in my mind. I replied out loud, "What you said about keeping hope alive is really true. I think a lot of my pain came from basing my hopes on people rather than putting them first in Christ."

"Well, Liz," Darren said with a laugh, "how would a child know that? You didn't seem to understand all that much about the Savior when I met you, let alone during your early years. Children naturally put their hope and faith and trust in their parents."

"You're right," I answered, grateful that he'd taken my side. "But it was a long time before I learned where I could safely realign my hopes when the others had failed me. Even though I didn't understand the principle of hope until years later, I think seeds of faith were being planted in me from the day I was baptized. That was the second time I'd received a spiritual witness I was able to recognize."

"What was the first time?" Darren asked, but I knew he'd already guessed.

"An answered prayer."

Darren's nod confirmed that he'd supposed right. "Ironic," he muttered, shaking his head, "that your greatest blessings came through your dad."

"Daddy filled my life with the worst misery a child can endure," I explained to Ben, "and yet through him came my only hope. Through him I discovered the gospel, and in it were the tools I needed to begin getting help."

"You mean the Church stepped in and played a part in leading your father to clean up his act?"

"Not exactly." I paused. "Unfortunately, almost not at all. I mean, it wasn't so much what the Church did for him but rather what the Church did for me. Daddy didn't let the gospel change his life the way it could have. But he did introduce me to the Church, and there, in the gospel of Jesus Christ, I found strength and hope and faith. That was where I gathered courage to go on."

"Can you give me an example? How did you gather courage?"

"Well, the atonement of Jesus Christ has been the greatest source of strength and hope in my life. I don't know if I can explain exactly how, because it has helped in so many ways, but take forgiveness as an example. There have been times when my whole being swelled up with hate and anger. Eventually I began to make a conscious effort to remember what had been good about my father. It was a real struggle, but I've done it." I took a deep breath, adding, "And as long as I'm being specific, remember that looking at what was good in my dad or forgiving his wrongs isn't the same as condoning them. I *do not* condone the things he did to Maria and me. But my efforts to forgive him have been greatly helped by the realization that through him God had meaning in my life."

Ben had been listening closely. "Not all abused women can say that, you know."

"No, of course not, but if they can, it will be something they can hold onto when it comes time to forgive. It will give them a place to begin."

Ben drew a deep breath. "And this courage and hope and strength began when you were baptized? How old were you?"

"I was eleven, but the faith didn't really come then. The seeds were just being planted. There had to be time for them to grow, and anyway, I didn't have the tools to harvest anything yet."

/ / / / /

The first of those tools was given to me at the time of my baptism. I'd enjoyed its help off and on before that day, but when I was confirmed, the bishop explained that I could now have this tool with me all the time if I was worthy. That was when Brother Rodriguez, a counselor in the bishopric, gave me the finest gift I have ever known: the gift of the Holy Ghost.

In spite of my claustrophobia, the confirmation was a supremely beautiful event. For the first time in my life, I had a name for my most trusted companion. This was my only true friend, the only one who had never deserted me. When I needed it most, that little voice had whispered for me to run. In quiet moments, it had wordlessly spoken peace to my heart. It had always spoken love. Now I knew why the voice was wiser than I was. I knew where it came from, and I knew how I could ask for its guidance.

If only I'd recognized the voice sooner . . . would things have been different?

"Come on!" Maria interrupted my thoughts by pulling on my arm. "The Primary president wants to see us."

Sister Cobbler, the Primary president who'd asked us our names the first day we'd gone to Daddy's church—our church, now—smiled as she hugged us. I could feel her love as she held out a white, leather-covered Bible to each of us. Our names were engraved on the bottom corners in gold.

Then Sister Benson of Benson's Laundry came over and hugged us. She had a matching Book of Mormon for Maria and one for me, with our names on the covers in the same lettering as the Bibles. But equally important, she'd written a pretty letter with her testimony on the inside.

/ / / / /

"Name some of the tools," Ben said.

"The gift of the Holy Ghost and the scriptures," I answered without hesitating. "Those were two great blessings that came to me on the day of my baptism. Without my father, I wouldn't have been there. Can you see how the Lord was kind to me through him?"

"The greatest good came right along with the greatest bad," Darren said.

"That's absolutely true," I said, smiling my appreciation at Darren. "An important part of trusting God and healing myself has been recognizing that blessings actually came into my life through my father."

"So birth would be another one?" Ben asked.

"Well, yes, that would be one for many women. But I was adopted." I paused before adding, "I have learned to thank my mother for the gift of life, though. Once I thought there was nothing to honor in either of my parents. Now I understand that isn't true—my mother gave me birth. And I guess, even as awful as mortality sometimes seems, if we shouted for joy over it in heaven, it must be a pretty big blessing."

"Mm-hm," Darren agreed. "I don't think we were entirely naive in the premortal world. I think we knew it wasn't going to be a picnic, yet we eagerly welcomed it and even fought for the privilege."

"I've known so many women who felt life was more of a curse than a gift," Ben commented sadly.

"I felt that way for a long time," I replied. "But the scriptures plainly say otherwise. I made a leap of faith and trusted them."

Ben silently considered what we'd said. "I want to talk more about what you just said about trust and the scriptures, but first, could I share a story with you?" We nodded, and he went on. "A woman I know told me something unusual once. She'd had a temple marriage, but a few years later her husband became abusive. Finally, she swallowed her pride and her fears and went for help. After the divorce, she remarried, this time to a convert. He is an exceptional man who has relied heavily on the Spirit in establishing relationships with her children. There were three girls and two boys—all somewhat confused because of the abuse that had gone on before the divorce. Anyway, she and her second husband were eventually sealed in the temple, and he wanted very much to adopt those children for eternity."

"Couldn't he?"

"No. A special letter from the prophet explained to this faithful woman that her sons and daughters had received some marvelous blessings in their birthright through their blood father. It doesn't take away anything from what a great man their stepfather is, but it shows that we can't see the whole picture from here."

"What could those blessings possibly be?" Darren asked.

"I'm not sure," Ben answered slowly. "I find it hard to imagine that anything good could come from such a man. But as we were just saying, there are things we can't see from this perspective. Perhaps some abusive fathers who haven't lived up to their potential have nevertheless given their children eternal birthright blessings we can't dream of. Perhaps there are blessings we can't see from where we are now."

"If you'd said that to me ten years ago, I might have spit in your face," I laughed, only half-joking.

"Yes," Ben answered, "it doesn't seem like much of a comfort when you haven't got a foundation of hope or trust on which to build faith."

"But look, here I am, listing blessings my father gave me."

Darren smiled broadly at me. Ten years ago, neither of us could have imagined saying these things—much less believing them. "One thing for certain," he said, with a touch of lopsided humor, "because of Liz's dad, our lives have been affected in ways I'd never have imagined."

/ / / / /

Obviously, Darren was right. My dad left an indelible imprint on who I am. Since my baptism, I have struggled to make sure that I determine who I am and who I will become. Baptism was an important part of that for me, as it was for Maria, too.

Maria became a different girl from that day on, too. I'm not sure exactly what happened. I knew I'd never be the same, but when I looked at her I had no idea how different she would become. Even the night of our baptism, she was suddenly vibrantly alive and much more outgoing with her friends.

From that moment forward, Maria was never my shadow again. In fact, she seemed to have pledged herself to be exactly the opposite.

/ / / 12 / / /

M om," I asked several weeks after our baptism, "how come you never had another baby?"

"Why should I?" Mom looked at me as if I were crazy.

"We don't have a brother, you know," Maria piped up from where she was bent over her homework. "All the other families at church have boys *and* girls in them—all except ours."

"Your father has not wanted another child yet, and I certainly am not ready."

"Ready for what?" I asked. All the ladies at church seemed to love babies. They always fussed and chattered over new ones.

"Ready to be stuck. Pregnancy is a nine-month commitment. You can't do much of anything, can't enjoy free time outdoors, and you're at the mercy of the baby." Mom's voice sounded funny, kind of sour and resentful. "Then, when it finally arrives, you're just beginning twenty years of worry and responsibility."

Maria's brown eyes were wide with hurt as she looked up at Mom. "Are you sorry you had us?"

"No," Mom answered, and her voice grew more normal. "No, I'm not sorry. I love you. But having another child is such a big commitment. I can't rush into something like that."

Can't rush. Who would ever believe it? Within two weeks Mom got really sick. She looked terrible. She was in the bathroom for days, throwing up and taking baths. She seldom came out.

Maria and I were smart enough to begin guessing what was going on. After all, we'd heard the jokes at church about the Primary fountain. All the Primary workers ribbed each other whenever they drank there because any lady who did seemed to get pregnant soon after that.

Mom's new job in the church was in the library, not the Primary, but Maria and I were sure she'd made the mistake of drinking water from that fountain. And our suspicions were verified within the week, when Mom went to the doctor.

"Have you seen the magazines Mom brought home?" Maria asked me with a knowing grin. "Definitely Primary water."

Sure enough, that evening Mom decided to break the big news. She was being so careful of her words and so mushy that Maria and I couldn't keep from giggling all over the place.

And the giggles didn't stop that night because Mom's belly began to grow like a balloon that was being blown up right before our eyes. She was always in the bathroom, and she was always crying over everything. Sometimes her attitude got exasperating, but most of the time it was just plain funny, uproariously funny.

That is, funny for us. Mom was miserable. By the time she went in for her second checkup, she looked six months pregnant. The doctor didn't think it was funny, either. Although X rays are dangerous for pregnant women, he scheduled her for tests.

Even then, Maria and I wondered what all the fuss was about. Pregnant moms always got fat. We didn't stop giggling until we saw Daddy pacing the floor all the next day, waiting for the lab to call with the test results. When the phone finally rang, it was only to explain that a specialist needed to be called in. Another day of waiting would have to pass before we could get the results.

That next day was one of the longest school days I could remember. It was one of the few times I ever ran home because I wanted to be there.

As Maria and I burst through the door, we immediately sensed a peculiar feeling in the front room. Mom was lying on the couch. Her face was red, her eyes were swollen, and her cheeks were glistening with tears. Daddy was standing in the middle of the room grinning from ear to ear. He had a giant manila envelope in his hands. "Well, Maureen, which one of us is going to tell the girls the news?"

Mom's voice was wavery. She twisted her wet hanky as she whispered, "You go ahead, Chuck."

Daddy pulled us over by the window and opened the giant envelope. "This is our copy of the X rays," he began. "Put your books down and get real close so you can see."

Then, pointing with his finger at the film, he showed us a white circle the size of a mayonnaise jar lid, with a five-inch chain of smaller white spots. "See this? It's the baby's spine. And look, here's its head and these are its legs. Can you see that?"

We both nodded. We could see the white places plainly, and they made sense once he'd explained what they were.

"See this?" Daddy asked, moving his finger to a different spot. "This is the other one's spine!"

Maria and I squealed. We jumped up and down. "Two babies!" we yelled in amazement and glee. Mom was having twins!

"Yes sirree," Daddy answered proudly. "This baby was hiding behind the other baby. When the doctor looked at the X rays, he wasn't sure if one baby had moved or if there were two of them. You can imagine why he was worried! He could only see one head and two spines. So then he called in a specialist." Daddy seemed very relieved as he smiled and added, "But the specialist said there are two—definitely two."

Maria and I began jumping up and down and yelling again, until Daddy put his hands on our shoulders. His face grew serious. Mom started crying again, choking on the sobs she was trying to hold back.

"Why are you crying?" I asked, going over to her and putting my hands on her arm. "Don't you want two babies?"

Mom only hiccoughed and cried harder.

"Mom's pregnancy is going to be very dangerous, now. She is in her later thirties and too little to carry two babies. If your mother isn't very, very careful, the babies will come too early. Early babies don't usually survive," Daddy explained, his voice trailing off.

"She'll be okay," Maria said brightly.

"Yes," Daddy answered. "She will. But we all need to help her. She had to quit her job today, and when she is six months along she'll need to go to bed for the rest of the pregnancy."

The full effect of those words didn't really reach Maria and me.

"Mom is going to need your help," Daddy said firmly.

Then I realized what was coming. I wanted to get angry—Maria and I already did more chores than any of our friends—but Mom looked so uncomfortable and Daddy looked sincerely worried. Besides, I was excited. Twins! Maria and I could get the work done.

Waiting for the babies to arrive wasn't the only exciting change in our family during the months that followed our baptism. Even more wonderful and bewildering than the twins were the changes in Daddy.

"You give it to him, Maria," I said emphatically one evening.

"Nope," my sister answered. "You're gonna have to." Then she suddenly paused. "What if he doesn't wanna go to our Daddy-Daughter Wild West Party?"

"Oh, he'll go," I answered with real assurance. "It's at the church." I was just hoping he'd keep his second face on. Neither Maria nor I wanted to be embarrassed among our new friends. He'd been wearing his church face all the time, though, and I felt more confident than ever before.

"Let's give it to him together," Maria said, clenching her fingers over my hand. But as we rounded the corner into the front room, we both stopped. Daddy was reading the newspaper. A sure way to goof things up would be to interrupt him, so we froze in our footsteps and tried to back out of the room.

The newspaper rattled. "What do you want?"

I gave Maria a shove; she was holding the invitation.

"Here," she said, pushing it into his lap. Then she turned around and ran, with me hot on her heels.

Later that evening Daddy came to our bedroom and leaned against our doorjamb, his thumbs hooked into his belt. A big grin was plastered across his face, and a black Stetson hung low over his brow. A light brown mustache had been drawn across his upper lip, and a bandanna circled his neck. Beneath his Levi's were snakeskin cowboy boots, complete with clinking spurs. Two gun belts circled his waist, a pistol at either hip, and on his chest shone a badge.

"Wal," he drawled, as if he were from Texas, "you two fillies reckon mah duds is fine enough fer y'all's hoedown?"

Maria and I gasped. "Sure," I said, struggling to keep from laughing. Neither of us had ever seen our dad look so ridiculous.

"Wal, then, it's all settled!" Daddy drawled through his grin. He pulled a pistol from its holster and spun it nonchalantly around his index finger. "You two half-pints'd better get yer ma to sew y'all up some fancy foofaraws so's yer costumes'll be as good as mine. I'll be here t' round y' up on time, an' I don' want no trouble. Y'hear?"

We heard! And our preparations kept us busy during the following week, but at last the night of the party came. Mom had sewn square-dancing skirts of gingham with three crinoline petticoats each for Maria and me. She combed our hair up fancy, tied in big gingham bows, and laced bright scarves around our necks. We were almost to the door when she came waddling out of the bathroom with a tube of fire-engine-red lipstick.

"Now you're ready," she said breathlessly.

"Darn tootin'!" Daddy beamed, taking each of us by the hand. His costume was the same as before, except for the addition of a vest and some fringed leather gloves. He even walked like a wild-west gunslinger.

Maria could contain herself no longer. "You look ridiculous, Dad!" she blurted, laughing. "You'd better take first prize with your costume! I don't think any of the other dads will get this fancy."

Daddy wasn't even annoyed. "No other hombre's gonna be this han'some, even if'n they tries," he nodded, tipping his Stetson a little lower. "I'm too good lookin'."

"Just don't bring 'em home too late, Sheriff Earp!" Mama said, collapsing on the couch.

With that, Daddy swung the door open for us to go out. This new side of him was taking some getting used to. I found it hard to think of him as the same monster who usually lived at our house. Maybe the old Daddy was gone for good.

That daddy-daughter party was a blast! We ran some gunny-sack and three-legged relay races, learned to do a square dance, and then shaved balloons covered with shaving cream. Daddy had to hold our balloon, and it was kind of scary when it popped. Little bits of shaving cream flew out and splattered all over him. He drew a very deep breath that made my heart thud with fear into the pit of my stomach. But then he only laughed—laughed and laughed. Maria and I laughed, too, giddy with relief. Maria was right about the other dads. They dressed up, but they just didn't compare to Daddy. He won the prize, and all evening the other dads kept making a game of trying to steal his fancy black hat.

Maria was proud of him. She and her friends were too wound up to eat, so they followed us outside and ran around playing tag while the rest of us ate watermelon. Daddy and I sat together, cross-legged in the grass, munching watermelon and seeing how far we could spit the seeds. After a while he nodded in Maria's direction. We both smiled. She was really enjoying her new status.

Maria and I had never had much free time, but after the party it grew even less. Mom couldn't do anything except go to the bathroom. If she pushed The Squid, she went into labor. If she fixed dinner, she went into labor. Whenever she went into labor, she cried. Whenever she got dressed, she cried. Her maternity clothes were almost too small, but she was too short to go up still another size. So she cried.

Maria and I were getting sick of all the extra work. Mom hovered over us because she had nothing else to do, and that made it worse. We couldn't satisfy her no matter how hard we tried. Yet we couldn't get mad at her because she always cried.

When the last day of school came, our friends were all set

loose for a summer of fun. But we went home to work. The doctor had put Mom to bed earlier than he had originally expected. She wasn't allowed to do anything at all. Daddy fixed the meals, and Maria and I did the housework and yardwork. Mom could never be alone, so Maria and I had to rotate our free time whenever Daddy was at work.

Mom was getting so big she couldn't get out of her chair or bed by herself. So every time she had to get up, she cried. The doctor laughed and said she was as big around as she was tall. Mom cried again. He said he'd make house calls for the rest of her pregnancy because it would be too stressful for her to come to his office. Of course, she cried some more.

To make matters worse, something the doctor called toxemia had set in. Mom began to swell like a balloon, so Daddy bought a massager. We spent a lot of time watching TV and massaging her feet for her because she could see them only when they were elevated. There were special pillows in every room for propping her feet up, and none of her food could have any salt in it.

Maria and I got a real kick out of watching her tummy. The babies were so wiggly you could see them move from across the room. "They're fighting for position," Mom said. "Usually you can't see babies move from so far away."

The summer dragged for everyone. There was so much work to do. Maria and I had to weed the garden every morning by nine o'clock. We had to edge the lawn and do the laundry. But Daddy's cooking was the worst of all. He became so frustrated that he soon wound down to a routine of hamburgers on the barbecue or scrambled eggs and toast.

"If I have to look at one more unsalted scrambled egg, I think I'll die," Mom groaned.

Maria whimpered, "Can't we have something else tonight?"

But Mom was resigned. "Daddy's doing the best he can."

"Couldn't you sit in the kitchen and tell him what to do?" I begged.

Mom's green eyes brightened. "That's a great idea! When he walks in the door, you two let me do the talking."

"No problem," Maria giggled. "If it means a decent dinner, I'll quit talking for a week."

The instant Daddy came home, Mom raised herself up on her elbow. "Chuck, how would you like enchiladas for dinner tonight?" She sounded so pitiful. "I've been craving them all day. I could walk you through it—it's real easy."

Maria and I looked at each other with raised eyebrows. Boy, was she smooth!

Daddy's voice was even more pitiful than Mom's had been. "Are you sure I wouldn't ruin them?" Even *he* knew he wasn't a good cook.

"You'll be fine," she beamed. But the next hour was far from smooth sailing. Daddy had a hard time keeping all the filling inside the tortillas. When the bottom end of one squirted meat and cheese all over the floor, Mom laughed. Then Daddy got mad. Real mad.

Mom had to do a lot of apologizing and showing how much she appreciated him. But when the enchiladas finally hit the table, complete with an unsalted serving for Mom, they tasted great. Still, Mom didn't think she could handle walking Daddy through it again. She said Daddy was worse than a blind armadillo in the kitchen. He'd made such a mess that just thinking about it made her cringe. Besides, she couldn't sit up like that again. So we ate burgers and scrambled eggs the rest of the summer.

Mom really was pretty bad off. Some women from the Relief Society threw a shower for her, and she couldn't even go to that. She refused to be seen in her pajamas, even though they were the only thing she could fit into by then. So her visiting teachers brought all the gifts to our house afterward.

We were delighted when school started again, but Daddy was almost frantic about leaving Mom home alone. He bought a fancy pager and a new phone for her nightstand. We fixed her a sack lunch every morning before we left and came straight home from school every afternoon. I began realizing that Mom had been right: nine months *is* a long time.

/ / / 13 / / /

Even a long, miserable pregnancy isn't a permanent condition. Despite all our efforts, the babies were finally on their way. Maria and I knew "premature" was something very dangerous, and we begged to go along to the hospital, but Daddy was adamant. So we went to school, where neither of us learned a thing. As soon as the bell rang, we ran for home. No one was there.

At last, at about four o'clock, Daddy burst through the door. "A boy and a girl!" he bellowed proudly. They were tiny and weak, so they'd need help breathing. Right now they were in intensive care, but the doctor said they were going to be just fine. And so would Mama, he added, sweeping us both off our feet for a hug. Charlene L. Hughes (he'd vowed the first would be named after him) had weighed in at barely four pounds. Vaughn B. Hughes had weighed two ounces more. We were lucky, he said, very lucky.

Then, somehow, we were supposed to go to sleep. Daddy explained that Grandma and Grandpa Hughes were going to pick us up the next day, feed us dinner, and take us to the hospital to see our new brother and sister.

I lay in bed dreaming about the babies. Mom's pregnancy had been a lot of work for everybody—and no eleven-year-old likes to lose free time—but I was beginning to think it had been a really great year. Even though we'd worked hard and done without some comforts (like good meals), we'd all been working together, and it had been fun.

I could hardly wait to see our twins. They were going to be rosy cheeked, curly haired, and stunningly beautiful. I knew it. And I was going to be a wonderful big sister.

A few weeks went by, and finally the babies reached a safe weight and gained strength. Maria and I could hardly contain ourselves the morning Mama announced they were coming home! They each had an I.D. picture, and a tag on one arm and one foot.

Mom left their arm tags on for a while, and I didn't blame her. With their diapers on, those two were identical. They didn't even have a distinguishing birthmark. Both had light brown peach fuzz on top of their heads and black, black eyes.

"Why are their eyes so dark?" I asked Mom, who was leaning back with her own eyes closed, attempting to sleep.

"The doctors put drops in their eyes so they wouldn't get infected. They'll turn back to their own color in a few weeks."

Daddy came into the room with his third or fourth load of things from the hospital. This time he had an armful of papers and two packs of diapers. "Where do you want these?"

Mom pointed across the room to the dresser. "That should be fine for now. I don't think the babies will be climbing for a little while yet."

Daddy stuck his tongue out at Mom teasingly. He'd been such a "nervous nellie" that he had actually baby-proofed the whole house before Mom even came home, weeks before the twins ever left the hospital. Funny things were stuck in all the outlets, hooks had been attached to the cupboards, and he had spent one morning crawling around the whole house on his knees picking up no-nos for babies. He couldn't seem to find enough ways to work off his excitement.

But while his energy had grown with his excitement, Mom seemed to have lost all of hers. She could hardly move. For the next couple of months we were constantly fetching diapers and bottles. Every three hours was feeding and changing time. The babies and Mom did nothing but eat and sleep. Nighttime was different, though. Sleep was out of the question because the babies, and therefore poor Mom, were up and down, up and down.

The fast Sunday after the twins came home was a great day for Daddy. He got to show off his babies and bless them in church. Grandpa and Grandma Hughes came, which was nice, everyone said, because they hadn't been to church for years. Grandpa said nothing had changed much, and he didn't seem very thrilled, but Daddy couldn't quit smiling. He even cried as he blessed his pretty little twins, all dressed up in white.

Looking back, I think fatherhood took on a new meaning for him that day. He was more sensitive after that. He even handed out compliments and was sometimes a little mushy. I'll never forget the night he came into our room at bedtime and told us he loved us. Just like that—out of the blue!

The next afternoon, Daddy was putting a load of diapers in the washer. I was in the upstairs bedroom.

"Liz!" Daddy hollered.

I thought he was going to tell me to hang a load of clean diapers out on the line, but I answered anyway, "What?"

"Could I speak to you for a minute?"

I ran down the stairs to the laundry room. "Yes, sir?"

"I have something important I want to ask you," Daddy said. "You seemed surprised when I told you I love you."

I was stunned. If I'd been caught off guard then, I nearly lost my teeth now. I never dreamed he'd draw attention to the moment when he'd gone soft.

"Don't you believe me? I love you and Maria just as much as I love these new babies. You're not afraid I'll love them more than I love you girls, are you?"

Daddy's questions were baffling. I'd never considered that he might love the twins more than us. To be honest, I'd never been quite sure he loved us at all. The only times he'd said so were when he wanted us to be adopted and when he wanted us to be baptized. I'd heard him say it a few times to other people, but I figured that's what grown-ups are supposed to say. And if it were true, well, he had a real weird way of showing it.

But this "I love you" had come when there was no one to impress and no ulterior motive. *Maybe . . . ,* a little part of me thought inside, *maybe he is finally figuring out what it really means to love someone.*

"Um," I answered, "it's just that you just don't say that very often. And about the babies, uh, well, all dads want their own kids, don't they? I mean, after all, we are adopted."

"No," he said gently. "You don't understand, Liz. Dads and moms love all their kids the same. I'm excited to have new babies of my own, but I would never give up you and Maria for anything in the world."

Now I was really confused. I knew this conversation had to be a result of our new religion, because it was so dedicated to families. Even in my Primary class they told us that family members should love each other the way Jesus loves us. I'd been amazed not only by how sure the people at church were about that but also by how easy it had been for me to believe it. The little voice inside me had whispered, *Yes, Elizabeth, this is true.*

The voice told me other things were true, too. I had felt so warm inside when I had learned that I am a child of God and that He loves me. Perhaps Daddy wasn't really going soft; maybe he was just realizing that little Elizabeth was also very important to Heavenly Father. Maybe the voice was talking to him, too!

Daddy reached his arms out toward me. I hesitated and then took a step forward. He gave me a great big hug—I think it was our first. "I guess I'll have to remember more often to tell you girls I love you," Daddy said. "It's important that you believe me."

/   /   /   /   /

"Daddy wasn't always awful," I said out loud. "There was a time when he really tried hard to be good to us. I think he did everything he knew of to be a model father, then."

Darren's eyebrows were raised. "It wasn't a very long time," he said.

"No, but I think he was sincere."

"Was that when you were baptized?" Ben asked.

"Well, yes, but I think the high point was when we went to the temple."

/ / / / /

"Hello," Bishop Kendall said. "Come in and have a seat."

Maria and I filed through the door first, followed by our parents, each carrying a three-month-old baby and its paraphernalia.

"I'd like to sit closer to you tonight," the bishop said as he pulled his chair around in front of his desk and smiled at Maria and me. "Do you know why we are here?"

"Don't you?" Maria asked. Her question wasn't disrespectful; she truly didn't know.

Daddy gasped. "We haven't told them! We wanted someone to help answer questions," he explained. "I knew I probably wouldn't have the right answers."

Bishop Kendall's smile grew even bigger. "Your daddy is very smart. And I can't tell you how happy I am to share this moment with your family."

The babies weren't so happy. Mama was getting embarrassed, but the bishop didn't seem to care. "Go ahead and lay them down on the floor to stretch," he said. "We've had a lot of babies in this office, and not one has ever wanted to sit and talk."

Mom and the babies were grateful, but the bishop's mind had already gone back to the matter at hand. "Your mother and father have decided to become an eternal family," he told Maria and me. He sounded very proud of them.

"What's that?" Maria's voice sang out, high and cheerful.

Bishop Kendall spent several minutes talking just with Maria and me, patiently explaining, answering questions.

I was shocked. The idea that we might not see each other in heaven was entirely new to me. I'd always assumed that if we all came from heaven, we'd all return there, too.

Maria and I didn't leave the bishop wondering how we felt about this decision. I mean, who would say no? No one in their right mind! Heaven, I reasoned, is better than earth, and things had been pretty great the last few months. The bishop was promising even better things. This was even more exciting than my baptism! We were finally becoming the wonderful family I'd been dreaming about for so long—just like the Waltons on TV.

"I know I'm forgetting something," Daddy muttered several days later, walking back and forth in the front room.

Mom handed him a fussy baby. "Here, hold Charlie while I finish combing Liz's hair."

Now Daddy and Charlene were walking back and forth. Maria was all ready to go, so she was playing with Vaughn on the floor. She looked extra pretty in her baptism dress. Daddy had his white pants and shirt in a bag to change into later, along with bags containing Mom's white dress and the babies' outfits they'd been blessed in.

"Behave!" Mom commanded my orange-red hair as if it were alive. People only rave about naturally curly hair if they've never tried to tame it.

"Come on, Maureen," Daddy called in the voice he used when he was trying to be patient.

Mom began caking on the hairspray. "He's forgetting to relax and enjoy his day," she whispered to me.

"Aren't you ready? I don't want to be late for this," Daddy said, coming to the bathroom door.

Charlie spit up. Mom produced a rag for mopping up father and daughter. "Yes, this is as good as it gets. I'll bring Vaughn." As she made her way into the front room, she said over her shoulder, "When have you ever been late for anything, anyway, Chuck?"

Maria and I each grabbed a diaper bag and then followed our parents out to the station wagon. Getting everyone buckled in was almost a ritual. "White clothes—check; babies' whites—check; bottles—check; diapers and wipes—check; recommend—Recommend! I knew I forgot something!"

Daddy hopped out of our station wagon and ran back into the house. Mom chuckled, but she sounded irritated. "I can't believe he forgot the recommend," she said.

Daddy ran back to the car, breathless. "Maureen! Do you

have your keys?" It was all Maria and I could do to keep from bursting out laughing. Mom reached into her purse and handed him her keys. She didn't say a word as he ran back to the front door. Pretty soon Daddy came bounding back. He leaped over the ornamental cactus patch in our front yard and into the car. I believe we exceeded the speed limit all the way, but we arrived at the temple on time.

As soon as we had pulled into a parking spot, Daddy began unloading everyone. Mom and Dad were getting things organized and Charlene and Vaughn were making noises, but the moment I looked at the temple, I was caught up into my own world.

Although we'd driven by the Arizona Temple many times before, it had never seemed quite this beautiful to me. Sunlight was teasing the leaves of the palm trees, glancing off the bright temple walls and dancing across the bas-relief sculptures that decorated them. It was such a lovely, sweet place that I even forgot to breathe.

"Come on," Maria said, tugging on my sleeve. "Don't stand there with your mouth open."

People in white welcomed us as soon as we stepped inside the big doors. Two grandmas were waiting to take the twins, and two more came forward to take Maria's and my hands. Mommy and Daddy would be busy with some very special things for some time, they explained. Meanwhile, we could stay in the children's waiting room.

What a wonderful place! There were cribs for babies to sleep in, play pens, toys, coloring books, and crayons—more than we could possibly do if we'd had all day.

It seemed like no time at all until another grandma in white asked us to get ready. Maria and I dressed the twins, while the grandmas smiled and exclaimed softly over how quick we were and what a good job we'd done.

Then we took an elevator that opened onto a very long hall. We passed many doors and lots of people dressed in white. The carpets were beautiful, the walls were beautiful, the furniture, the lights, the flowers—everything! But I was marveling at more than the beauty I could see. I knew this place was holy. Everyone we passed looked happy. No one had to tell us to whisper—we felt the reverence inside ourselves. We felt the peace.

The grandma holding my hand stopped in front of a big door. Gently she swung it open, and I saw a room filled with familiar faces. The whole ward must have been packed in there! Mommy and Daddy were in the center of the room, holding hands and waiting for us.

I had never, never, ever seen such a beautiful place. The chandelier was made of tiny dangling pieces of glass, and its brightness glittered everywhere. I couldn't express the awe I felt, but I knew this was a place where truth and love flowed freely, like pure water. Like the light from that chandelier.

I just stood there, the wonder of it all washing over me.

The grandma holding my hand led me forward and showed me where to kneel at the altar. Maria followed, and two ladies in white assisted the twins. We all held hands.

My deepest wish was coming true! All my secret dreams, so precious I'd hardly dared think them, were becoming reality. This was the most happily-ever-after fairy tale I could imagine, yet it was immeasurably more significant, more real, more lasting.

A very kind man in white began talking to us. I wasn't sure whether I was supposed to close my eyes, but I didn't. I couldn't take them off what was around me. I couldn't take them off my daddy. Tears were streaming down his face. Mom had bowed her head low and was very still. The twins were awake but quiet. Maria and I threw smiles at each other.

Everyone in the room suddenly whispered amen, and I realized I hadn't heard a word the man had been saying. "Amen," Maria and I echoed.

Then the man asked us to stand together and look into one of the mirrors that hung on all the walls. There was our family going on and on in the reflections: Mama and Daddy each holding a twin, Maria and I on either side.

We are an eternal family, my heart sang. I was so happy I felt as if I were floating.

The man explained to us that if we lived the best we could and repented when we made mistakes, our family could go on forever, just like the reflections. On and on and on and on . . .

Daddy squeezed Mama and kissed the top of her head. He bent down and lifted Maria off her feet in a hug. Then, turning toward me, Daddy knelt and gave me a tremendous, yet gentle hug. "I LOVE YOU," he said.

/ / / 14 / / /

Our future looked so perfect when we went to the temple. God had answered my prayers—we really seemed to have become the wonderful family of my dreams."

"What went wrong?" Ben asked.

Darren's arm around my waist squeezed a little tighter. "I've wondered the same thing for years," I answered with a sigh. "I was so young. It was all so confusing."

"Have you ever talked with your parents about it?"

"Oh yes, I've talked with Mom many times."

"And did she give you answers?"

"Yes, but they have never made any sense to me." Ben was waiting for me to go on, so I took a deep breath. "I think the answers to my questions—questions that I asked of my mother, of Darren, of God—never made sense because I was asking the wrong questions."

"What kind of questions?"

"For years I asked, What did I do wrong? Why was Heavenly Father mad at me? Why did I deserve this? Was I an awful person?"

"Oh, I see," Ben breathed.

"Only recently have I understood that what happened was a result of people making choices and acting on their own decisions. God was *not* punishing me. What happened was *not* a reflection of my value in His eyes."

"You're right, Elizabeth." Ben spoke gently but with conviction. "The Lord has told us over and over that He wouldn't put us in any situation without also giving us what we need to overcome our challenges. He must have a lot of faith in you to believe that you could be in this family and still return to Him. It takes a lot of strength to break the chains of an abusive cycle."

/ / / / /

"I'm never going back!" my mother yelled as she went running into the house. "If all you Mormons want to live like hypocrites, you can. If those other women are stupid idiots, so be it!" She threw a diaper bag down onto the couch, pulled off her high heels, and stomped toward her bedroom. At the entry to the hall she stopped and turned around. "I am not going to be sucked so far into this that I can't get out! I'm a whole person. I think for myself and refuse to be at your mercy. I don't need a man to tell me when I may breathe!"

"What?" Daddy stood in the front doorway. His face was blank and pale with shock. "What are you talking about, Maureen?" He took a few steps forward and held out his hands.

"Don't play ignorant with me!" Mom growled defiantly from across the room. "I found out what you men do during priesthood meeting." Her voice was almost hysterical. "I can't believe I almost fell for it!" Then she turned, and her green eyes sparked. "If you think you're going to keep me barefoot and pregnant, waiting to ask how high you want me to jump, then get used to disappointment, Charles Hughes!"

"Maureen, you don't understand something. I'm sure that's not what it means." Standing on the porch, looking in through the screen door, I was astonished by the sound of Daddy's voice. He seemed confused but genuinely concerned. He wasn't answering Mom's anger with anger but with love. "Give me a chance to explain, Maureen."

Mom shook her head violently.

"Whoever you've been talking with is misinformed."

" 'Whoever' is right here in these books," Mom said, stalking over to the locked cupboard in the china cabinet and pulling out five or six paperbacks. "Not just one book, Chuck, but many, written by women just like me. These are women who tried desperately to make their failing marriages work. They tried to keep their husbands happy, while those selfish men went right on manipulating them!"

Mom's voice was high, pinched with emotion. She shouted at Daddy for hours, but not a word of it made sense to Maria or me. She kept repeating the letters *ERA* and words like *self-fulfillment,* but we couldn't figure out what it all meant. Finally, we went around to the back door and slipped upstairs into our bedroom. Below us, we heard the babies cry and get fed, we heard doors slam and bang, and we heard Mom yell. I'm still amazed by Daddy's patience that night. He'd never allowed anyone to speak to him in that tone of voice. In the past, if Mom had ever gotten even remotely angry, he'd verbally put her in her place at once. She'd always kept her mouth shut at his command.

Over the next few months, things got more and more foggy. Eventually, I began putting two and two together, but I didn't like what they added up to, and I hoped I was wrong. I prayed I was wrong.

My dream was crumbling right before my eyes. I felt betrayed. *God, where are you?* my heart screamed.

Maria and I kept going to church with Daddy. One Sunday Sister Dobson taught us that if you pray with only righteous desires, your prayers will be answered. She told us faith could move mountains. Well, my desires were righteous, and I had a lot of faith. I wasn't asking for any mountains to be moved, only for a happy family. I wasn't asking for anything God hadn't given other people.

I tried to hold onto the dream, but it slipped through my fingers. I even asked Mom some point-blank questions. She gave me answers I couldn't understand, but I knew she'd interpreted things from the temple session to mean she was less valuable than Daddy. "Why should he be my boss?" she demanded. "I am just as good a person—even better! And I've never done some of the awful things he has."

After her first big blowup, the fits of pettiness grew in violence and frequency. She quit going to church, and she made a lot of changes that suggested she was becoming more and more convinced she'd made the wrong choice in going to Daddy's church.

For example, she'd always disliked the modest dress code Latter-day Saints voluntarily practice, but now she violated it flagrantly. "Whoever made that up," she announced, "did NOT live in Arizona!" And under her breath she muttered about some conspiracy to make women feel unattractive. She read a put-down for women into every little thing anyone said or did. She told us the scriptures have two meanings: the right one, and the one husbands want their wives to believe. Pretty soon she had an impressive list of things that Daddy and his priesthood buddies were going to do to their wives—and she was quick to recite it.

I began to disbelieve my mom. It was that little voice again, whispering, *Be patient. Your mom loves you. But she doesn't understand.*

/ / / / /

Ben said it took strength to break the chains of the cycle of abuse. I wished God hadn't thought I was up to it! There were so many chains . . .

"Chains," I echoed my thoughts out loud. "Our house was full of them. Chains of physical abuse and sexual perversion were inflicted on me by my father." Compared with the memories, my voice seemed distant. "But Mom did her part as well. She was bound with chains of mistrust and fear and cynicism. She left the Church without knowing whether it was true. She joined as a sacrifice for her family, but she turned away and chose to believe what deceitful people said about the doctrine."

"She never had a testimony of her own?"

"No." I looked down. "That's how everything beautiful began to fall apart."

It still hurt to think about it, and by their silence, I knew Darren and Ben could tell. If you've tasted both the good life and the bad life, why would you choose to go back to the bad? Why? I had always figured there were things Mom didn't tell me, but only in the past year or two have I come to understand what some of those things were. After she married Daddy, Mom discovered that Grandpa Hughes had been abusive—perniciously abusive. He'd even attacked Mom sexually once while he was staying in our home. She wanted to trust Daddy and believe he'd moved beyond the problems his father and grandfather had, but she was paralyzed by confusion and fear.

Worst of all, Mom had quit believing in God years before. She had nowhere to turn, no one she could ultimately trust. When she was only five years old, both of her parents had died in a car crash. My mom had been taught that God answers all prayers, and she'd taken that promise literally. So she'd knelt down and prayed for hours in her closet, but her mom and dad never came back. After that, she quit believing in God and His love. Every time something awful happened to her—and plenty of awful things did—she saw each new incident as proof that God wasn't real. She kept telling herself that a loving Father in Heaven would never let such things happen.

"Time has revealed things about my Mom that have given me insight into the way she acted," I told Ben. "But that information didn't come when I was desperate to get it. If I'd understood her long ago, everything would have been so much easier."

"Did you have to work your way through love and forgiveness first?" Ben asked, then smiled understandingly when I nodded. "I'm glad you got the insights, even though they seem late. It isn't easy to accept that there are things we may never know about certain people in this life. But we *can* determine the way we will act and feel toward them rather than being slaves to what they do."

"You're saying act, not react—right?" Darren broke in.

"Exactly," Ben said.

I understood the principle they were talking about. In fact, it has been an important factor in discovering how to move on with my life. But that doesn't deny how hard it was to take control and act independently upon my own future. It doesn't deny how horribly I suffered before I found the way to change things.

To my twelve-year-old eyes, it seemed as if Mom had pulled her finger from the dike and thumbed her nose at the rest of us. No matter how hard we tried to stop all the little insidious trickles, the entire dam was sure to fall. And when it did, the filthy flood crashed over us all.

/ / / / /

Shortly after the babies were born and not long before we went to the temple, our home became a three-ring circus: Daddy decided he would go to college and improve himself.

He was miserable at his job. Other people got promotions before he did just because they had some little slip of paper called a diploma, not because of their work. So Daddy left the post office and began going to school full time. Meanwhile, until graduation, the bishop said that he and Mom could work for the Church as regular staff at the Bishops' Storehouse. And Mom, to our surprise, agreed to go back to church in the name of a brighter future.

I, too, was having my own new educational experiences. That was the year I started junior high. My new school was much larger than the old elementary, and there were students attending from four other elementaries, so I made many new friends.

Teri and I didn't have classes together anymore. We saw each other at church, but with all the changes, my best friend soon became Rosa. She was the zany, bubbly, Latin beauty who first talked me into trying out for swing choir.

In junior high, we were still pretty much little kids, afraid to touch hands with our partners and uncertain about doing even the most simple dance steps. But there were a few girls who had taken tap and ballet lessons, and that gave them an edge. Never having had any training, I could only rely on the quality of my voice and my eagerness to get involved. Not until I'd committed myself for tryouts did I realize how stiff my competition would be. That was when Daddy came to my rescue by teaching me some dance steps.

He got out his old records and showed me the basics to all the routines. He coached me on how to smile and when to breathe and taught me other fundamentals of stage presence. Daddy even got acquainted with the choir director and volunteered to chaperon our first road trip.

Daddy seemed even more excited about my being selected than I was. In my opinion, the entire experience was a kick, and I was pleasantly surprised by the way things worked out. But what really meant a lot to me was the way Daddy cared. Throughout the rest of that first season, He would ask me to do a shuffle-step-kick or sing a difficult harmony as if it were our own private joke. Maybe I remember that period of my life in a rosy light because that was one of the last times he relaxed with me, cared specifically about me, and had a good time.

He carried such a heavy credit load at the university that his teachers came right out and told him he was nuts. They accused him of trying suicide by college burnout. But Daddy was under too much pressure to take things slowly.

Mom wanted more money. She took another job working nights. That way she could work at the Bishops' Storehouse all morning while the twins played beside her in a playpen. Daddy unloaded trucks and did paperwork during the morning. Then, when Maria and I came home from school, Dad took off for night classes and Mom left the babies with us while she went to her other job.

Daddy was becoming a very irritable person again. We tiptoed around whenever he wasn't in class because the littlest noises made him angry when he was trying to study. Daddy had a phobia about tests, so he had to work extra hard to remember things. He memorized information forward and backward. Even years later, not only could he answer the questions from his freshman classes but he also could tell you exactly which book and page to find those answers on. That's how he maintained his 3.8 grade-point average.

During the first quarter Daddy took a self-awareness class

that led him to tape up recipe cards all over the house. They said little things he wanted to remember, such as, "Stand tall and confident," "Stay one step ahead of the others," and "Winners sit at the front." He worked at applying those principles in his own life and vigorously encouraged us to implement them as well.

So, off our family marched to the front of the chapel every Sunday (at first with Mom, later without her and the twins). And maybe Daddy was right when he said you learn more at the front. At least, I was learning things that were going to be very important for the rest of my life.

One time my Sunday School teacher taught about the Creation. At the end of the lesson, she gave each of us a picture of a slightly clumsy ballerina standing at the exercise barre and looking into the mirror, where her reflection shone in a perfect image of grace and poise. Across the bottom of the picture were the words "God don't make no junk."

I figured this quotation was just as valuable as one of Daddy's cards—but this one was mine. Something told me it was absolutely true and tremendously important. When I got home, I colored the picture and taped it up on my bedroom mirror. It hung there for years.

The day I brought home that picture, its meaning burned deep within me. But in the successive waves of confusion that washed over our family, I discovered that I had to sit very still on my bed to remember the warm feeling it had given me when I'd first seen it. Why weren't we trying to be a celestial family anymore? What had I done wrong to lose my dream-come-true?

Everyday living was much harder now. The heartaches hurt even more than the first ones I'd experienced as a little child. I knew things didn't have to be this way.

"Mom, can I ask you something?" I scooted up beside where she was folding laundry and started in on some diapers.

Mom didn't even look up, but I was getting used to that by now. It seemed she and Daddy had forgotten how to smile or even how to say hi. We kids just seemed to be in their way.

"Mom, do you and Daddy hate me?"

That got her attention, but she went on folding as she answered in a scolding voice. "No, Liz! Of course not."

"Well, then, why are you always yelling at me? Why isn't anything I do good enough for you and Daddy?"

I wanted her to hug me, but instead I got an even angrier response. "You know we love you, Liz. We just don't like the things you do."

"Why does everyone have to yell about everything?" I was crying now.

"We have a lot of stress, and that's what makes us yell," Mom said matter-of-factly. "We don't like our life the way it is right now, and we're working very hard to make it better."

That seemed like a dumb answer to me, so I left and went to my room. I thought things had been better than they'd ever been before, until Daddy quit his job and Mom quit the Church. I didn't see any need for all this change to come ripping through our world. I tried to talk about my feelings only a few more times. More and more questions gathered in my heart, but the answers Mom gave seemed to get dumber and dumber.

/ / / 15 / / /

School once again became my escape from reality. As the mood around our house steadily declined, I began participating in as many extracurricular activities as I could. I tried out for the swim team and made it. I practiced day and night to make it into the high school swing choir (they took lots of road trips!) and signed up as a volunteer aide in the office so I could go to school early once a week.

On Friday nights and Saturdays I worked to pay for my choir trips, choir clothing, and swim gear by tending children. On weeknights Maria and I were baby-sitters, housekeepers, and full-time students. When we weren't grounded, we went to MIA. When we were grounded, we lost all our telephone privileges, had to stay home from church, and couldn't take baby-sitting jobs. That made it hard for me to earn enough money to pay for my school activities.

School offered less of an escape for Maria. She wasn't doing very well, and she began changing her circle of friends. "Losers" and "undesirables," Mom called them, but Maria didn't pay any attention. These were kids who didn't care if she got a 3.0 or if she couldn't get out of the house. They couldn't, either.

Vacation days were soon upon us. "This summer isn't going to be easy," Mom said, referring to the third job she'd taken when school got out. "But once I land a permanent spot with the hospital instead of this part-time one" (she was a front-desk receptionist and after-hours answering service), "I'll quit the others."

I soon went back to worrying about when the next beating would be. Daddy had begun hitting us again, but not with the kind of blows that left really bad bruises—at least on the outside.

/ / / / /

"Daddy! Daddy! Come home!"

"What's the matter, Maria?" I could hear his voice through the telephone receiver. "Just tell me."

"You know the swamp cooler on the roof?" Maria paused to hear his answer. "Well, something's wrong, and water's leaking all over our bedroom! The carpet's all squishy and wet on one side."

Daddy came home and looked things over. He turned the swamp cooler off and told us to gather everything up and stack it all on the dry side of the room. Then he went back to the Bishops' Storehouse, where he and Mom were trying to finish inventorying a truckload of items that had come in that day.

Maria and I worked for hours, taking apart our beds and pushing our heavy dresser against the other wall. All the little things got stacked on top in total chaos.

When Daddy finally came home that night, he was too tired to look at the problem even though everyone was hot. Maria and I slept on the Hide-a-bed in the TV room and got up early to search for our Sunday clothes.

"I'm not going to church today, girls. I'd better stay home and try to fix the cooler," Daddy said, coming upstairs a few minutes before Sunday School. He exploded as he came through the door. "What the heck is this mess?" he yelled. He began chucking things at us. "You're a couple of real slobs!"

Maria and I started to cry. "We did the best we could, Daddy," I said, furious even in my fear. "The furniture was heavy. We didn't think it had to be done neatly, just quickly, before it got wet."

Daddy made a simpery face and used a whiny voice. "We did the best we could," he mimicked with disgust. "You should've been raised in a barn. You're a pair of *pigs!*" He threw my jewelry box, and it broke against the other wall. Then he did the same with my porcelain vase. "Yeah, that's a real good idea. In a barn . . . " he growled, grabbing us.

Clenching our hair in each of his hands, he dragged us downstairs and through the kitchen to the back door. As he pushed us out the door, he kicked us both in the rear, sending us tumbling to the pavement. Maria's dress tore; her arm was bleeding.

"Get your faces out of my sight! And don't ever come back!" he yelled. "I told you I wouldn't let pigs in my house. Go find some dump to live in!" Daddy slammed the door and locked us out.

Maria and I ran. We didn't even know where we were going. We just ran and ran, tears streaming down our faces.

"Liz," Maria coughed at last, choking for air between sobbing and running. She was holding her side. "Where are we going to go?"

Her words stopped me in the middle of the sidewalk. I stood there for a long time, looking at her, my own shoulders heaving with each breath. I began a desperate inventory of all my friends. Finally, I thought of something worth saying. "Let's go to Lonnie's. I've known her since kindergarten, and her mom hates Daddy. Lonnie told me just last week that she couldn't believe he—"

I broke off midsentence because Maria had quit sobbing long enough to look at me. Her eyes were big and round and void of hope. I wasn't very convinced, either—we both remembered too well our experience after going to Andy's house—but Maria didn't have anything better to offer. Most of her new friends had parents like Daddy.

"I wish I could keep you girls," Lonnie's mom said when we finished telling her what had happened to us that day and in the past. "Let's call the police and say you are runaways. When you tell them you want assistance, they'll investigate your father and nail him to the wall. What he's done to you two is illegal."

So we phoned, and the next thing we knew, we were

placed in a foster home to wait for a hearing. That home was the filthiest place I'd ever seen. Neither of the parents had jobs; they just lived off the money they received for doing foster care. Although they weren't mean, they weren't friendly, either. Until Lonnie gave us each a change of clothes, we hadn't had anything except the Sunday dresses on our backs, and they were getting dirty quick in that house.

We had to wait three days for our hearing. On the appointed morning we got up early, put on our dresses, and stood by the window until the attorney came to get us. She arrived three hours late, with bad news.

"Hi there," the attorney said, smiling. She was a young woman with mousy brown hair and tiny eyes that hid behind a pair of round glasses. "There's been a change of plan. Your dad has plea-bargained. That means he pleaded guilty to the charges against him, and since it's his first offense—"

"It is *not!*" I shrieked in terror. "He's been doing it for years! We told you that!"

The attorney was very calm. She cleared her throat and clarified, "This is the first time your father has been brought to court for his actions. The judge was lenient because he had never been in court before and because he pleaded guilty. A social worker will be coming into your home for the next few months. If there are any more problems, she will help you take care of them."

"Is she gonna live with us?" Maria asked.

"No."

"Then what good's she gonna be? He'll just hide it like he always has. He'll wait until she's gone. She'll never know."

"You have to tell her. She is there to protect you."

"What if we refuse to go home?" I asked, folding my arms defensively.

"You don't have that choice," the attorney said, squelching my brave stand. "The judge says you must."

We walked through the front door of a house that felt colder and darker than ever before. Mom stayed in her room. Daddy looked at us with contempt and told us to get cleaned up.

Our bedroom was exactly as we'd left it. The carpet was dry and matted; the ceiling and one wall had water damage all over them. Broken things were still lying on the floor where Daddy had thrown them. We cleaned up what was ruined and put everything else away. Mom didn't speak a single word to us for days, but Daddy had plenty to say during dinner.

"When I showed the judge my picture of your filthy pig-pen, I told him, 'This is what I have to put up with all the time.' And you know what? He felt sorry for *me,* not you! You think you're so picked on, but he didn't even care."

Daddy was apparently enjoying his food. He chewed with gusto and took a second serving while everyone else was still struggling to force down the first bite. "Well, now you're back, but that's only because I said I would take you back. So listen up. If you want to be out on the streets like bag ladies—or dead—just squeal one time to our social worker. Tell her how mean I am and how I hate you. I guarantee you won't ever open your mouths to anyone again!"

Maria and I got the message loud and clear.

We lied to our social worker during the months that followed. Maria admitted to being lazy at school and said she would start trying. I confessed to being a mouthy, hot-tempered brat who tried to make trouble. I voluntarily promised to obey and honor my parents as the scriptures tell us we should. Daddy said he would be more patient with our many imperfections, and Mom stated over and over that she didn't have any problems.

One day the social worker quit coming. She had officially labeled our family rehabilitated and functioning.

/ / / / /

"You do have to take control of your own life," I told Ben. "But that isn't an easy thing to do, especially while you're living at home."

"I didn't say it was." He put up both hands in innocence. "There are ways and means available to help, though."

"That's true." I was ready to let his comment alone, but Darren spoke up.

"The first time Liz ran away, the adults she turned to for help immediately phoned her dad to come get her. Going home was a terrible, painful experience."

Remembering the beating I'd had, I wondered how those strong words *terrible* and *painful* could sound like such a measly understatement.

"Did you ever try to get help from someone who was qualified?" Ben asked me.

"Like turning myself over to the police?"

"That would be one way," he said, looking at me closely. "I see you did. And things didn't get better?"

"Is living in fear of your life an improvement?"

Ben nodded again and sighed. "Just this week I was reading about this problem in a Denver newspaper. The title of the article was 'Aurora Gets Tough on Batterers,' but from what I've read and from what women like you have told me, I'm not sure *tough* is the right word."

"How's that?" Darren asked.

"Well, in all fairness, most of the cases that don't end in a guilty plea do wind up with a conviction. But what concerns me is that roughly one-third of the offenders plead guilty within the first twenty-four hours."[1]

"Like my dad," I said softly. "Then they're free to run straight home and do it again."

"I guess that's exactly what worried me. Abusers realize that plea-bargaining is an easy way out. All too often, it becomes a loophole for slipping through the fingers of justice."

Ben's words described Daddy's situation perfectly. And once you've gotten away with something, it becomes easier to do it again.

Daddy had turned back into the angry, foul-mouthed, destructive man of a few years before. But this time he was even uglier. Now he was wearing a suit on Sundays and exuding a wonderful-person, great-father image. He was becoming comfortable living a monstrous lie.

Horrified, I watched as Satan slowly, subtly clamped my family in his "awful" and "everlasting chains." I am an eyewitness to how he cheats men's souls and stirs them up to anger. I know that's how he leads them, one step at a time, "carefully down to hell."[2]

NOTES

1. *Rocky Mountain News,* 19 Mar. 1992, p. 8. "Special Report: Domestic Violence and the Courts, Aurora Gets Tough on Batterers."

2. 2 Nephi 28:19–23.

/ / / 16 / / /

Nephi describes Satan's chains. He explains how at first that great deceiver uses nothing more than a "flaxen cord." Because his victim isn't struggling to get away, one little flaxen cord is plenty. But by the time the poor slave discovers his bondage, strong chains have been locked into place.

That's what I saw with Daddy. I didn't understand it then, but the passing years and studying the scriptures and many, many prayers have made things clearer. With time, I've begun to sort out what was once a holocaust of confusion.

Making sense of what happened next in my life began when I realized this simple fact: an abuser is seeking control.

Daddy had been seeking control until the judge handed it to him on a lovely silver platter. He interpreted the court's dismissal as an encouraging pat on the back. "No problem, Chuck. You're doing fine," the situation seemed to say. And in the new light of what had just happened, Daddy saw control as nothing more than a toy. Power was what real men wanted. When Daddy decided he wanted it too, he voluntarily upgraded those flaxen cords to iron bands.

/ / / / /

There had been some rapid changes in our house once Daddy quit his job. But after Maria and I turned ourselves in to the police, things really sped up. Mom became different, too.

For one thing, her hair color kept changing. Now she was a

124

pencil-woven blonde—and every bit as beautiful as she had been when her hair was long and auburn, or layered and jet black, or shoulder length and frosted. I'd become used to frequent changes in Mom's hair color and makeup over the last few years, but there was something else I couldn't put my finger on. She didn't seem like my mother anymore.

One conspicuous difference was that she seemed so full of energy in spite of the many hours she was working. Hers was a strange kind of energy. It was tainted by an angry, belligerent attitude one moment and a boisterous, loud-joking, and crude personality the next. About a year later, I caught her popping pills and began to understand her moodiness. She'd been using drugs to stay awake.

I have never understood what happened to Daddy, though. Things had been miserable when he'd had two faces, but I never dreamed he would add a third face to his wardrobe.

There was the good-father look he wore on Sundays, though he'd mothballed that one around the house. Then there was the mean, angry, physically and verbally abusive face that I was seeing more and more often. But along came a third face that I'd seen only twice before—both times in the toolshed. Manipulative, peculiar . . . The lips on this face said 'I love you,' but the eyes terrified me beyond words.

/ / / / /

Coming home from swim practice one evening, I found Maria crying. She was sitting alone in the dark, in our bedroom with most of her clothes off.

"What's wrong?" I asked, flopping down beside her and handing her a blanket off the end of the bed.

"I . . . I'm . . . not sure." She was still in the hiccoughing stage of grief, trying to bring her silent sobs under control.

"Then why are you crying?" I worked on getting her to look at me. "Why?"

She turned away. When I put my hand on her shoulder, Maria shrugged it off. "Don't touch me!" Her words were terse, anxious. "I'm just scared. That's all. *Scared to death*. I don't want to be alone in this house anymore."

"Maria, what happened?"

"I'm not sure!" Her confusion and anxiety exploded. "That's just the problem. I wish I knew!" Then, drawing a deep breath, she added cryptically, "Whatever it was, it wasn't good."

"Come off it!" I was irritated by her babbling; this seemed to be just another of her vague explanations. "Spit it out, for once. Make a little sense!"

Maria was staring at me, her round brown eyes brimming with fresh tears.

I softened my voice. "Start at the beginning, and speak clearly."

After a minute, Maria wiped her nose and swallowed hard. "I was here, at my desk, doing my homework, when Daddy came in our room. He started asking me questions about what we'd done at the Beehive party. I didn't know why he was here, Liz! He was staring at me in a strange way. It was so scary!"

Maria lunged to her feet and walked across the room, twisting her hands together. "The next thing I know, I'm here, lying on the floor, Liz. And where," she wailed, "WHERE are the rest of my clothes?"

"Well, now, my dear," I began trying to laugh away this absurdity, "if YOU don't know how your clothes came off, who does?"

"Exactly!" she whispered, her words bouncing around the walls of our room like cannon fire. She stopped walking and leaned, sort of huddled up, in her corner, staring off into space. I wanted to get up and run somewhere far away, to shout, to scream, to break something, to laugh and laugh and laugh—to do anything! But I couldn't move.

All at once Maria turned on me, angry. "I don't want to be home alone with Daddy anymore, Liz. Ever since I was little, I haven't been able to remember my times tables around him. I've never been able to do my chores well enough to please him. And now . . . now . . . " Her bottom lip began to quiver, and her voice cracked. "Now I can't even remember what I've been doing for the past two hours!" Her voice was so low I could hardly make out the words. "Something's very wrong, Liz. Something . . . I don't understand," her voice dropped away entirely.

This all seemed far-fetched to me. "What are you trying to say, Maria? Can't remember? That's ridiculous!"

At the impatience in my voice, Maria broke down completely. She slumped onto the floor and started sobbing. "I don't know how it could have happened, or . . . if . . . or . . . I just don't know, Liz . . . "

"Know what, Maria? What?"

"It's spooky, Liz. I think he's driving me insane!"

I turned away and noticed her clothes, heaped on the floor behind the door. My stomach lurched, and I came abruptly to my feet. "Maybe you passed out."

"I don't know," Maria moaned. "I just don't know."

"Well, I don't either!" My frustration blared through the crossness of my voice. "Don't go anywhere near him, okay? Do your homework in the twins' room or something."

"How's that going to help, Liz?" she whined, looking at me as if I were off my rocker. "How—?"

I didn't know what to think; the whole thing was weird. Exasperated and confused, I jumped up and stormed out of the room.

Now I was the one wearing blinders. I knew what might have happened, but somehow I denied my suspicions—and yet I didn't, not completely. Instead, I focused on what seemed like the distant future. Someday I'd be able to go away on my own. When I turned eighteen, I'd be legally free to get out of there. That was only four years away . . . four years.

/ / / / /

"Hi, Liz," Daddy said one early evening in October. "What are you up to?"

As I looked into that eerie I-love-you face, I answered, "Watching TV." Inside, I was thinking he'd just asked a really dumb question. Quickly turning back to the screen, I tried to lose myself in an episode of "M*A*S*H."

"Oh," Daddy said, sitting down on the floor beside me, a "Fashion Duds" bag in his hand. "You sure look good in those shorts. Your legs have such a nice tan, Liz, especially for a red-head. You must have spent a lot of time outside last summer."

"Yep," I replied, without following his gaze to my white shorts. Of course I had. Maria and I did all the yard work around our house. *When I turn eighteen, the dumb questions and the yardwork will all be behind me,* I thought eagerly, burying myself in Hawkeye's troubles at the mess hall.

"I'll bet you look real good in a swimsuit," he murmured.

I pretended to be totally engrossed in my show.

"You sure do have some strong-looking legs, Liz."

"Swim team helps," I said politely, realizing he wasn't going to be ignored. "We work out a lot."

Casually, he pulled a black, french-cut suit with a zipper front from the bag he'd been carrying. "Why don't we try this new one on you? I'd like to see you in it."

Maria's tearful words flared across my mind. Several weeks had passed since then; I'd almost forgotten it. Inside me, the familiar voice was screaming, *Be careful, Liz. Don't trust him, Liz.*

"Nah," I answered warily, "It's not my style."

Daddy's laugh sounded like a snort. "Hah! Girls like you don't need to be modest, Liz. Black's going to look striking against that nice tan and foxy red hair of yours. Show me, okay?"

"No," I said flatly, turning back to "M*A*S*H" again. But I couldn't get a handle on what was happening. That was the first time I'd ever turned down a new swimsuit. I could really use one, and my funds were low right then. But something inside me was firmly insisting that I shouldn't touch this suit, not even for a million dollars!

Mentally, I fumbled for an excuse to leave. A commercial . . . I started hoping for a commercial. Maybe I could say I had to go finish my homework. The next few moments crawled by slowly. I began praying the phone would ring or Maria would come home—anything!

I felt Daddy's hand slide up and down my leg. "I sure am proud of you, Liz. You're a real sharp girl." His fingertips went up under the hem of my shorts. "I'm glad you're doing so well at—Gee, Liz! You sure are soft."

I glared up at him. Heat and anger filled my face. I wanted to scream at him to get his hands off me, but my mouth wouldn't work.

Daddy quickly moved his hand to my back and patted me as if I were one of the guys. "Now where was I before you sidetracked me?"

I wanted to yell at him, *"I sidetracked you?"* but my mouth was still stuck.

"Oh yes . . . swimming. I'll have to squeeze one of your meets into my schedule some time."

Daddy didn't speak for several minutes. He seemed absorbed in the television program, but his hands weren't so interested in the comedy.

Awful memories flooded over me. Maria's voice kept saying, "I don't know, I don't know . . . " I remembered the toolshed . . . sitting on my bed . . . shivering with fright.

"You sick pervert!" I heard myself yell. I was standing on my feet, screaming. "Keep your hands off me! I hate you! Just stay away from me!" Then I was running to the bathroom. I locked the door behind me. Maria and I had been told never to do that, but I didn't even hesitate.

Daddy banged on the door. "Let me in, Liz. I'm sorry. It's not what you think. Please, Liz, let me explain." He coaxed and begged, sounding deceitful and desperate.

Don't open that door, Liz, the voice inside me said. *No matter what, don't open that door.*

Then I remembered the extra key on top of the door frame. He only had to look up . . .

Please, please don't let him find it, I prayed. I climbed into the linen closet and shut the door. The closet was very large, stretching all along one wall beneath the eaves of the roof, so I wiggled between towels and bedding all the way into the back corner.

I'm not sure how long I was there or how long it was before Daddy went away. My mind was frozen to the point where I couldn't even think . . .

"Open the stupid door, Liz." I suddenly realized Maria was yelling. "You're not funny."

Crawling out through all the towels, I wondered when she'd come home. "Sorry," I said as I turned the knob. "My stomach's upset."

I'm not sure why I lied. I never told Maria what had happened to me that day. I didn't tell anyone for years. I was too ashamed. I felt filthy. And the words Daddy had used continued to haunt me in nightmares: "YOU side-tracked me . . . YOU side-tracked me . . . It's not what you think. . . ." Sometimes I began to wonder if I was crazy. Was that day my fault?

/ / / / /

"The abuse itself isn't really the biggest problem," I told Ben. "Confusion is."

"Explain."

"Well, when a perpetrator thinks he's getting away with something he knows is wrong, he begins to rationalize. He begins to confuse right and wrong—or at least he tries to."

Ben nodded but didn't speak.

"But what's worse is how his confusion can spill over into the mind of the victim."

"Yes," he said. "I know that's true. The first step toward healing is for victims to understand and really believe that they are not guilty for what another person has done." He paused and repeated, "Confusion . . . " Then, realizing Darren and I were looking at him, Ben clarified, "Sometimes—with good intentions—a girl will put herself between an abuser and her siblings to protect them, or throw herself at her abuser because she thinks she is keeping the family together, or respond favorably in a desperate search for love and acceptance."

Darren spoke up. "It's important to remember that all those situations can be worked out with a priesthood leader. No abuse victim has to stay buried under feelings of guilt, whether they're self-imposed or real." Ben nodded as Darren went on. "Elder Scott's conference address made a point of explaining that 'no matter what degree of responsibility [is involved], from absolutely none to increasing consent, the healing power of the atonement of Jesus Christ can provide a complete cure.' "[1]

Darren's words were particularly meaningful to me because I knew of the time when he'd worked through his own repentance with a priesthood leader's help. He knew the pain as well as the joy that follows. Still, I didn't want to be misunderstood.

"That sounds so simple," I broke in. "And it is. But when you're caught in a cesspool, nothing seems simple. The abuser has power over you, and you're stunned."

"Elder Scott mentioned that, too," Darren said. "He said most victims are 'innocent because of being disabled by fear or the power or authority of the offender.' "

"I'm grateful to know that now. But at the time I felt so dirty and polluted. I really wondered if it *was* all my fault."

"You said earlier that the Holy Ghost helped you whenever you would listen," Ben prodded. "Did the Spirit help you with those feelings?"

"Well," I paused. "Yes. Yes, but not the way you're thinking. You see, my feelings of dirtiness, although they seemed like a torment, were actually a blessing. They kept my resolve strong. At least, no matter how confused I was, they still told me right from wrong. I always knew when Daddy had done something bad. And I was very blessed in my situation, because I was old enough to fight off his advances."

"But you still felt confused and at fault," Darren said.

"Oh, yes! My fear of the sexual advances was so great that I couldn't really even think about it. But violence was something I'd been living with for years, and I could handle that. So I concentrated on my fear that he would physically hurt me."

"Not on the sexual abuse," Ben echoed.

"No. It was only years later, when Darren and I were married, that I began to understand. Then, when Darren used some of the touch-words Daddy had used, they triggered something awful inside me. The confusion drowned me again, and I began to realize how deeply Daddy's abuse had affected me."

"So getting help to clarify the confusion is a very important part of getting away from the abuse and moving on," Ben said.

"Yes," I said emphatically. "Very important."

NOTE

1. Richard G. Scott, "Healing the Tragic Scars of Abuse," *Ensign*, May 1992, p. 32.

/ / / 17 / / /

N
o one can clear up that much confusion by themselves," I
told Ben.

"No," he answered. "That's why people who have been
abused are always counseled to get help—to keep asking, yelling, screaming for help until they get it."

"We're back to that?" Darren said. "I know of four instances
where Liz went to someone in authority over her. Things only
got worse."

"Yes, they did," I agreed. "But I could have kept on asking
for help, instead of giving up each time."

"Right, Liz," my husband said with gentle sarcasm. "When
we met, you were paralyzed by your fear of that man."

"Absolutely!" I admitted. "But things are different from how
they used to be. People are more aware that abuse exists. They
aren't as disbelieving, and they know more about what to do."

Ben was looking at me intently, as if he agreed with what I'd
said but was wondering whether I really meant it.

If only he knew how hard it had been for me to understand
that fact. I knew the hurt of asking for help and receiving nothing. But I've also had to live with the realization that I could have
kept screaming until the fire got put out. Maybe, if I'd done that,
things would have ended differently.

/ / / / /

"Who was in the TV room last night?" Daddy demanded

133

from the door of our bedroom where we were getting ready for school.

"I was," I said, wondering frantically what I'd done wrong. My beatings seemed to have been getting closer and closer together these days; they seemed to come for no reason at all.

"You left a filthy bowl of half-eaten potato chips by the couch! How many times do you have to be told to put things away, you stupid pig!" Daddy turned on his heel and marched downstairs, growling obscenities.

"I'm sure I put that away. Besides, I wouldn't leave my bowl out and not my glass," I muttered, looking at Maria. "He's full of it!"

"So what's new?" She shrugged in apathetic disgust.

Maria seemed as if nothing could touch her. That must have been because of the crowd she was hanging around with at school, I reasoned. She'd entirely quit caring about her grades anymore.

After her fiasco with the special education reading program, Daddy had given up on her. He ignored her feelings as if she were a worthless loser. Though her report card beatings had stopped, I could tell his obvious disgust struck Maria worse than any blow. Perhaps that was why at the last minute before grades came out, Maria would turn on the tears and tell her teachers she was trying so hard, that it just wasn't fair. When they wouldn't change an F, she used a typewriter and changed it into a B herself and then did the same with her grade-point average.

My thoughts suddenly jerked back to the present as Daddy came stomping up the stairs again. "Do you think I'm going to put it away for you?" Suddenly he reached down, jerked off his shoe, and began swinging it. That hurt as much as the Ping-Pong paddle he'd used the last time, or the hairbrush the time before, only now he kept hitting me across my back instead of my behind, sometimes missing and striking my arm. Then he threw away the shoe, doubled up his fist, and hit me with all his strength, several times, tossing me around like a rag doll. Suddenly the room began spinning and grew dark. I'm not sure if I actually fainted, but I know I collapsed on the floor.

As soon as he was gone, Maria pulled me to my feet. "Hurry," she whispered, very close to my ear. "Go put it away."

The stairway seemed like a descent into the pit of doom. I paused at the bottom, taking a deep breath before starting down the hall. I kept ducking, certain that Daddy would be lurking around one of the corners. But he wasn't. Snatching up the bowl, I hurried into the kitchen, poured the leftover chips into a plastic bag, and put the bowl in the dishwasher. Then I met Maria by the front door, where she had brought my school bag.

I cried all the way to school. My back and bottom burned wherever my clothes rubbed against the welts. My chair stung. We had to shower after P. E., but I managed to get one of the private stalls. The warm water felt so good on my welts that I let down and cried again.

After a while I realized someone might hear me, so I quickly washed off my makeup and hurried to my locker to dress. The rest of the class was waiting by the doors to be dismissed.

When the bell rang I knew I was going to be late, so I tried to hurry. But as I pulled the door open to leave, my gym teacher grabbed me by the shoulder. Her touch almost sent me flying through the ceiling with pain.

"Liz," she said, "you're wanted in the office."

"Me?" My stomach lurched. "What . . . what for? I've never been called into the office."

"I'm not sure," she said, with a face that gave away nothing. "Here's a pink slip."

I worried all the way down the hall, my stomach twisted in knots.

Mr. Fiero, the school police officer, greeted me as I stepped through the door. Both he and his partner were very friendly; they asked me to come into their office.

The next thing I knew, I was being searched and asked endless questions. Would I please pull up the back of my shirt?

I was humiliated.

"We won't hurt you," the officers kept reassuring me. They promised I would be okay.

Beyond my humiliation lay confusion. Whenever Daddy

hadn't been angry with me during the last few months, he'd made sexual advances. I didn't know how much I'd been doing wrong, or what was my fault. I only knew I felt dirty, dirty, dirty.

One night I'd awakened out of deep sleep to find Daddy standing at the foot of our bed. Since then, it had happened often, and sometimes the blankets had been pulled down. Fear began ruling my life in a new way: I stopped wearing shortie nighties and sleeping soundly. I told Maria that even though it was hot, we couldn't sleep in just our underwear anymore.

I was lost in shame and confusion as the school police pulled up my shirt and examined my back.

Tears streamed down my face once more. "Please," I choked on my sobs. "Please don't make me talk anymore, Officer Fiero. I'll only get in trouble. I already told the police the truth, but the judge sent me back home anyway. I can't go through that another time."

"Your dad won't ever do this again," Officer Fiero said. "Your dad will never know you told us anything."

I finally gave in and answered all their questions. Then they stepped out of the room and allowed me a few minutes to pull myself together. I was supposed to return immediately to class, but on the way I stopped in the bathroom and threw up. I was so sick—sick with terror and humiliation.

Hunched over the toilet in that dimly lit, graffiti-scrawled bathroom, I finally gave up. I simply didn't care whether I lived or died. Leaning my head against the cold tiles on the wall, I wished with all my soul that I could just fade away.

/ / / / /

"You went for help four times?" Ben asked.

I nodded.

"Once to a friend's house, once to the police, and then where?"

"One of my teachers turned me over to the school police because of some welts on my back," I said.

"And you were examined?"

"Yes, but nothing happened. I waited for the beating that I

knew would end my life, but nothing happened at all. I guess they never did anything about it."

"Can I read you something?" Ben asked, leafing through his planner. "Speaking of physical, psychological, and sexual abuse, President Monson said: 'When you and I know of such conduct and fail to take action to eradicate it, we become part of the problem. We share part of the guilt. We experience part of the punishment.' "[1]

The room was silent for a moment, each of us pondering the forceful words Ben had just read. "You know what?" I broke the silence at last. "President Monson's statement supports what I was saying earlier. That a member of the First Presidency is speaking boldly about abuse can give hope to victims. Nobody ever talked about these things when I was little. I was married before I ever heard the words *child molestation*. The very fact it had a name made me feel vindicated and relieved some of the confusion in my mind."

"Yes," Ben agreed. "Abuse is an ugly subject, but hiding the realities that do exist won't make anything better." After a moment's pause he said, "So you actually talked to the police twice. What was the fourth place you turned to?"

This was going to be awkward. I didn't want to give him the wrong idea, so I didn't answer right away.

"Her bishop," Darren said. "Liz's bishop called her into his office one night before Mutual. He explained that he'd heard there were some serious problems in her home, and he told her he wanted to help."

/ / / / /

When I heard the bishop's words, instant fear swept over my body. Daddy's sexual advances were increasing, but there had been fewer beatings lately. Time had only been intensifying the chaos in my mind.

There was no way I could tell this man the truth. He worked with my dad every Sunday, because Daddy was the executive secretary. I knew I'd be making a big mistake if Daddy ever found out I'd said anything to the bishop.

"I . . . I'm sure . . . sure things are going to get b-b-better real soon, Bishop," I stammered. I didn't want to confess to anything. I didn't know what I should confess to. "Daddy is going to be graduating, and he'll be getting a good job soon."

"Liz, I wish I could believe that. But the problems I'm concerned about won't be solved by a job."

I was sweating all over and cold. Did he know what went on at our house? How? If I lied to the bishop, I knew God would punish me. Although I wasn't so sure anymore that there was a God, I didn't want to find out the hard way.

In spite of my confusion, I'd always continued attending church. Perhaps the inner voice was urging me to go. Somehow I knew my only safety was in that place. And now my fear was erasing the security I'd felt.

The bishop moved over next to me and sat in the chair at my side. "It's okay, Liz. My responsibility is to help the members of the ward, the way a father does. Let me help you, too."

A father? Like I wanted another father! I didn't know what to do. Why couldn't I run away?

Hesitantly, I started talking. I knew bishops were supposed to keep confidences. With tears washing my face, I began to tell about some of the beatings—but I didn't tell all of it. I never even hinted at that third face, that really scary side of my daddy.

I couldn't tell what the little voice inside wanted me to do. It seemed as if I should talk, but I was afraid to really open up. "Please don't tell Daddy I said anything," I pleaded. "Please. I'm afraid he'll kill me."

I was remembering Officer Fiero. It was painful to think he hadn't acted on what I'd told him and what he'd seen that day. So I concluded that he understood how, if he interfered, my situation would get worse. I even told the bishop about that humiliating experience. I hoped he would see my situation the same way.

The bishop smiled and told me not to worry. Because those had been Officer Fiero's same words, I assumed nothing would come of all this. I went home to bed thinking that I had only two years left before I turned eighteen. Maybe I really could survive two more years. . . .

The back door slammed, waking me from my sleep. Daddy's feet pounded up the stairs. Suddenly I was flying through the air. Daddy had pulled me right out of my bed by the front of my flannel nightgown.

"Well, I understand you have been running off with that big mouth of yours again, Liz. I've warned you for years that it was going to get you in trouble. You didn't listen. So tonight I'll just have to prove it to you."

The next thing I knew Daddy's fist was hitting my face. He was screaming, but I couldn't hear the words. He kicked me and punched me and picked me up and threw me across the room several times.

After the first few moments, I couldn't feel a thing. I was only an emotionless witness to the events. Later, I discovered a burning sensation. Hot tears were running down my cheeks, but the only feeling I had was an intense determination never to tell anyone anything again.

I stayed in my room, pretty much in my bed, for three days. I was so banged up, I could hardly move. Although I somehow managed to do my chores, I didn't go out until I could disguise my face with makeup. I didn't see or talk to anybody. No one was going to know or guess about my life. I wasn't trusting anyone ever again.

NOTE

1. Thomas S. Monson, "Precious Children—A Gift from God," *Ensign,* Nov. 1991, p. 69.

/ / / 18 / / /

So your bishop called you in, and what happened?" Ben asked.

"I guess he had a talk with my dad after that. Then, when Daddy got home, he beat me severely." The room was very quiet again as Ben considered my story. "I should have taken those bruises down the street and shown the bishop or the stake president," I continued. "I never should have quit showing them until I got help."

"Come on, Liz," Darren said impatiently. "You were so confused and scared. Get help—ha! You were focused on survival. Don't blame yourself for how you reacted."

"You're right. I can't change things now, and I don't carry guilt around over it. But if I were in that situation today, that's what I would do. I'd yell and scream and tell the whole world my story until someone paid attention. I'd get help, and I'd get out of the confusion."

Darren was halfway incredulous. "How could you have gone back to the bishop? You've told me how you didn't think you could ever trust anybody again."

"But, Darren," I said, "I *could* have gone back to the bishop. You see, I didn't tell him everything. He chastised Daddy according to what he knew. If I'd told him the whole truth, he might never have sent me back into that situation."

"I see," Darren said. "If you'd asked for the help when you

were still bruised and extremely frightened, it would have provided a lot more support for what you were saying."

"No doubt that's true," Ben put in, "but let's don't forget there have also been great changes in the last ten years. There's a growing awareness of abuse. Church leaders are speaking out against this crime, and that's not all. Leadership training meetings are being held, with the support of LDS Social Services, to help bishops and auxiliary leaders. Bishops' handbooks specify the Church's standing on abuse and contain guidelines for both the perpetrator and the victim. Our own stake president has spoken out against all forms of abuse. He's promised that if injured persons will only ask, he'll give them aid."

"The problem is the asking," Darren said.

"I know!" Ben answered. "But requesting help allows civil authorities and church leaders to step in. If they're not asked, they can't do as much, often nothing at all."

Ben was right, and I knew it. "If I'd told at the top of my lungs—no matter how afraid I was—I might have begun breaking the chain right then. Instead, I unwittingly perpetuated it."

Darren was watching me closely again. He's always careful to warn me about not carrying guilt for things I have no control over. But I was sure of myself and what I was trying to explain. So I went on: "Not only did the chains still shackle my dad, but they slipped even tighter around me. When I vowed I would not trust, I set myself up for Satan. It was a natural reaction, and it was the one he wanted. Soon, in my desire to escape my misery, I voluntarily took Old Slick's flaxen cord and looped it around my own neck. I got hooked on the bottle."

/ / / / /

Daddy's graduation finally came, but to my dismay, it didn't change a thing. In fact, the troubles in our home grew as the big day approached. My parents were always fighting. At the time, I couldn't figure out why, but now I think I understand—at least in part—what was going on.

Mom had been working all those jobs while Daddy was in school because she was hoping for better days to come. When

Daddy graduated with his pre-law degree, he applied to several law schools but received one rejection after another. No one could explain why; he was at the very top of his class. When Mom suggested it was his age, he was not only disappointed but annoyed, too.

Almost immediately, he took a job with a trucking company that paid less than his Post Office job had before college. He wanted our family to move to Texas, where the trucking service was based.

But Mom had worked hard to get her position as a full-time receptionist at the hospital. After taxes, her paychecks were now fatter than Daddy's. Besides, she repeated, this was the first real independence she'd ever had in her life. And just when she was discovering that she could choose for herself, she had discovered something else. From what I've been able to put together, and from an old letter Maria found, it seems that this was the time Mom discovered that Daddy had been having an affair. No wonder they fought!

Night after night, Maria and I lay in our bed, listening to their violent arguments. Several times, we ran next door to the Bensons' house to phone the police. Whenever the Bensons weren't home, we ran two blocks to a busy street and flagged down the first police car that passed.

One night, Mom and Daddy were in the pantry, shouting at each other. Mom kept yelling that she didn't have to put up with him anymore, and Daddy went on trying to put her in her place. Now, our pantry was so small that when two people were in there, one of them had to have been crammed halfway onto one of the shelves. So when I heard a tremendous crash, I thought Daddy must either have begun throwing all the cans and other things off the shelves or shoved Mom into them, causing a collapse. Once again, I ran to the Bensons'.

The police came and threw Daddy out. Mom had a nasty cut above her eyebrow and a badly bruised shoulder. She was really shaken up, but she absolutely refused to sign the officers' papers. She had never signed when they wanted her to, and of course, without formal charges, the police could do almost nothing. Mom was confused, too.

Just like always, ten minutes after they were gone, Daddy was banging on the back door and crying and shouting. "Maureen, please let me in . . . I'm sorry . . . I promise I won't hurt you anymore . . . I love you, Maureen. I can't live without you . . . I know I need help, and I promise I'll do better. I just don't know what's wrong with me."

About this time, Mom couldn't stand for the neighbors to hear all the stuff Daddy was howling about. She always let him back in, and he slept on the sofa. But no matter how hard Mom tried to keep things quiet, the poison sloshed onto our other relationships, too.

"I'm sick of everything," I told my friend Rosa one day as we were walking home from school. Though I'd never alluded to what happened to me when Daddy was wearing his third face, she knew about my beatings.

"I don't know what I can do to help you," Rosa answered.

"No one can help," I said. "But somehow—even if it's just for a minute or two—it feels good to talk about it. If you weren't around . . . well, I'm afraid I'd explode."

"Speaking of your home life, Liz, we really need to talk."

I gave her my full attention. "Sure."

"Well, Liz . . . Ah . . . I don't really want to dump on you, . . . but my parents say I have to."

I knew what Rosa's next words were going to be. Every friend I'd ever had—girls and boys—had sooner or later given me the same line.

"Liz, your dad scares me. I'm sorry, but I told my folks. I just couldn't keep your secret anymore." Rosa kept running on and on in my silence. "They don't want me to get involved. So, . . . well, we can't be best buddies anymore, Liz. I just can't deal with it."

Fighting back my tears, I spoke like a woman of steel. "That's okay, Rosa. I know where you're coming from."

Rosa sniffled, and I knew she was crying even though she was looking at her feet.

"It's okay. Really. We'll just be acquaintances, and that way you won't get in trouble with your mom and dad."

"I'm really sorry, Liz."

"See you around," I said, afraid to stay a moment longer. She reached out to touch my arm, but I couldn't stand it. "I've gotta go now, Rosa. I'd hate to get grounded again."

One by one, my friends fell away. Only Teri was left. She was too poor to go anywhere, and I was always grounded, so we had a comfortable, casual relationship. But in reality, I was very lonely.

One day I was running an errand for my algebra teacher during class, when I passed Maria and her friends in the hall. They weren't in high school yet, so I was doubly surprised. "Maria, what are you doing here?"

"Just skipping a stupid class."

"Why would you do that?" I asked. "What if you get caught?"

Maria's laugh was boisterous and invincible. "Get caught by who? *You* won't nark, and the school will never catch on unless I miss class more than once a week or have ten unexcused absences. And *that* won't happen."

Her friends were all laughing with her—not happy laughter but the snide, smirking kind. Anita, the leader of Maria's bunch (we didn't call them gangs, but this was as close as any group came back then) stepped right in front of me.

"Listen," she said in a cool, superior voice. "Let's shake the straight chick. If I were you, Maria, I'd never let anyone know she was related to me. It can bruise a girl's image, if you know what I mean."

I had no other methods for dealing with this situation than the ones I'd seen used in my home. So I used them.

"Who are you calling a straight chick?" I said, determined not to let anyone appear to have anything over on me. "I'll give you a run for your money any day."

For all my tough words, I was scared to death inside. I knew Anita enjoyed overpowering people, and I was afraid of being pushed around. I lived in a situation I couldn't fight, but I figured I could knock Anita around pretty good.

What I didn't realize was that Anita didn't want to fight. She had another, more clever idea. "Okay, Goody Two-Shoes. You're on. There's a party tonight at the park. Be there."

Maria didn't want to be embarrassed by me. "That's perfect," she said quickly. "She'll be there, and I will, too." I don't think Maria really liked her rude friend; perhaps she was simply afraid not to align herself with someone who seemed so powerful. In any case, she tauntingly added, "I do believe you're in for a big surprise, 'Nita. Huh, Liz?"

"Yeah," I said, stiffening up. "She sure is."

Maria talked Mom into letting us ride our bikes to the park that night. Mom was always so tired after work that the twins were about all she could handle. She was a real pushover now that Daddy was home from his trucking job only on weekends.

The kids at the party surprised me. No one ever picked the fight I was looking for. They just talked tough and drank a lot. I didn't want to appear wimpy, so I joined in. I even joined in a beer-guzzling contest and did very well.

Several guys at the party seemed impressed by my looks and my bravado. They laughed and joked with me, and I drank some more with them. I felt a lot less shy in their company than with the nice young men I'd known before. These guys couldn't discover anything about me that would shame me—I knew they were no better.

Although I left Anita's party very drunk, I managed to look stable on my feet and to keep from throwing up. My mother never had a clue about what I'd done.

And the next morning at school, I discovered I had a whole new set of friends. The day before, I wouldn't have wanted to be seen with them, but now it didn't matter. They'd accepted me, and I'd had fun showing off. I couldn't wait to party again.

After that, alcohol provided a wonderful escape from my frustrations, but I knew I had to keep my drinking a secret. I became very good at covering up. I even managed to drink before I went to school in the mornings and to sneak spiked Cokes into class.

Because I never skipped class or openly challenged authority, because I kept my grades up and my mouth shut, I never got into trouble. And I spent so much time concentrating on my secret that there wasn't much energy left to worry about Daddy.

/ / / 19 / / /

So your rebellion was drinking?" Ben asked.

"Rebellion?" I asked. "Well, yes, I suppose. But alcohol was much more than that. It was an escape, a relief, almost a consolation. Booze gave me a way to feel tricky—to hold something over on people who were holding so much over on me."

"How do you mean?"

"Well, they never knew. It was my secret, my private power. For once, I was in control."

"Chains of control," Darren said under his breath, and I knew he was thinking how Daddy's grabbing for control had left us all trying to grasp hold of some, too.

Ben didn't respond to Darren. "A book I read years ago contained one sentence that hit me like lightning. Since then, I have seen it verified time and time again in my medical practice. The concept was how rarely we find drug addicts and alcoholics among those who had previously always been normal, well-adjusted people."

Darren was looking quizzically at Ben, and I suppose my face didn't look much calmer. I was thinking how often people use addictions as a crutch and how I didn't ever want to fuel that fire.

"Don't misunderstand me," Ben said, chuckling. "What I mean is that certain behaviors such as drinking, doing drugs, or promiscuity are not the actual problem. They're symptoms of a deeper need for healing. They show us that something else is out of balance. If I understand correctly, in Liz's case, her drinking was an attempt to be free—even if only briefly—from confusion."

"That's right," I said, thinking about how useless it had been for me to struggle to gain control over my life and then turn around and throw it into a bottle.

"And," Ben went on, "there were probably other symptoms that grew out of the abusive cycle in your family."

I looked closely into Ben's face again and said, "Yes! Those chains really galled us! We struggled with alcoholism, loss of chastity, even—even suicide. But I want you to know something, Ben. I want you to know that the Lord never deserted me. In the deepest pit of my life, down in the depths of the worst blackness I can remember, God did not forget me. I thought He had. In fact, I was sure of it. But that was when, through His mercy, someone new walked into my life." I squeezed Darren's hand, struggling vainly to fight back tears and keep my voice steady.

I could see I was making Darren uncomfortable, so I joked a little. "Oh, he was human, all right. But he was like a savior to me. He exhibited one characteristic I hadn't known before, and that was love. Selfless, honest, Christlike love."

/   /   /   /   /

Even before school got out the year I was sixteen, I knew this summer would be different from any other summer. Maria got a job with Youth Alternatives, working to clean up some inner-city neighborhoods in Las Vegas. By an all-out miracle, I was able to land a job that also met my imposed obligation to care for the twins: I worked for a day-care center tending children while their parents took desert tours. But most important, Daddy was on the road five days a week.

"Where are you going tonight, Mom?" I asked, sliding around the corner into her bedroom.

She didn't even stop singing, as her voice swept along in a

beautiful soprano above the country-western beat. "Out," she sang with a big smile, fastening on a turquoise necklace.

Daddy wasn't home, but this was obviously something more than a trip to the grocery store. "Where?" I sang back, intentionally off-key.

"Just out," she grinned and turned away, but I wasn't giving up.

"With who?"

"Some ladies from work."

"Who? I didn't know you had lady friends at work. You're always telling me how you have to be so careful to stay above the office politics and produce enough paperwork to cover your own backside."

"That's right. I don't trust anyone; I don't help anyone. But that's during office hours. After work, the rules change." She smiled at me again. "Liz, I've really been looking forward to going out—I haven't been out in years. You *will* baby-sit for me, won't you?"

"Oh, sure," I answered. "But where are you going?"

"I think we'll grab a bite to eat, and then we might go out for a drink."

Mom's candor shocked me so much that I turned away.

"Liz, will you do me a real big favor? If Daddy happens to call, just tell him I went shopping." I must have had a funny look on my face because Mom sighed and offered a second option. "Okay, if you don't want to do that, just tell him you don't know. All right? I'm tired of your dad smothering me."

Fortunately for me, Daddy didn't call that night. And when Mom came in, her eyes were all lit up like candles on a birthday cake. "Have a good time, Mom?"

"You bet!" she said, with enthusiasm I hadn't heard before. "We had fun and went out for drinks. I got asked to dance several times. It was great!" I must have been staring again because she glared at me. "Your dad's an awful dancer, you know."

My mind dashed back over the lessons Daddy had given me, the routines he'd helped me decipher, the stage presence he'd helped me create. But an even greater jolt had stunned my senses. Flabbergasted, I blurted out, "You're not supposed to dance with other guys, Mom. You're married."

"Well, maybe not for long," she answered back smugly, her green eyes glinting. "If your dad won't give me a divorce, I may just have to force him."

I sneaked a drink just before crawling into bed that night. Shock from what my mother had said was still ringing in my ears. But soon I realized that her new attitude was reality. She continued going out a couple of times each week. And I wasn't as lucky as the first time, because sometimes Daddy called.

"Where is she?" he always demanded. "It's too late to be shopping. She should be home. Where'd she go, Liz?" When the answers I'd been instructed to give didn't satisfy him, he'd curse at me and slam down the receiver.

Then once Mom breezed in the door, there were always plots and questions: "Liz, do you think I'm making the right decision?" "Liz, it might put us in a slight financial strain if I divorce your dad." "You won't be angry, will you, Liz?"

I didn't want to be my mom's marriage counselor. I didn't want to be scared to death anymore, either. Why couldn't we ever have just one weekend without screaming and hitting? Why couldn't we have that happy family of my dreams?

Deep down I knew my wish would never come true. When the twins were asleep and Mom was still out on the town, I'd sometimes slip upstairs into my bedroom and stare at that ballerina picture with the caption, "God don't make no junk." *Maybe God doesn't love me after all,* I thought. *He doesn't answer my prayers anymore.* It seemed obvious that the biggest, longest, deepest desire of my life was never going to happen.

I continued sipping my secret elixir whenever I could get away with it. My other pastime was dreaming about the only wonderful thing in my life. During the days, the twins and I went to work at the day-care center, and from my first morning on the job, my eye had been fixed on a remarkable guy. Sometimes he drove one of the tour buses, and sometimes he worked as a wrangler for the more rough-and-ready desert tours.

It was completely out of character for me even to allow

myself to get interested in him. This guy was nice. He came from a good LDS family, and his values showed in everything he did, from his walk and his mannerisms to the way he paid attention to the little children we were taking care of. He was easily six feet tall, with muscular shoulders and legs, sun-bleached hair, and a dark tan. Most of the athletes I knew liked the rugged, wild, dangerous look, but this man was the clean-cut missionary type.

Stop! I told myself firmly. *That kind of hunk would never give you the time of day.* Besides, the humiliation of Daddy's alienating all my dates had caused me to swear off the opposite sex.

Daddy really had me on edge about guys. Whenever he was home for the weekend, he sought opportunities to question my knowledge of the facts of life. He asked explicit, filthy questions and wouldn't accept anything but a direct answer. For him, this was a game, a challenge to see if he could get me to respond without delicacy or discretion. I was always totally humiliated—which delighted him.

No wonder I was intimidated by the opposite sex! Still, something inside me persisted in thinking about the handsome guy at work. I found myself trying to think up ways to coax such a bashful, strong-and-silent-type to ask me out. Although Darren often gave us a ride home from the day-care program, I eventually began to realize that a full-fledged date might never happen.

One afternoon, as we pulled up in front of the house, I saw Daddy's Trans Am in the driveway. *Oh no!* I thought. Daddy wasn't supposed to come home in the middle of the week. I quickly said good-bye to Darren and hurried the twins in the door.

Mom was sitting alone in the front room, crying. When she saw me, she grabbed her purse and hollered upstairs, "Chuck!" Then she turned to me. "Liz, your dad and I are going to Vegas to get Maria. There's a leftover casserole in the icebox, or hot dogs, if you'd rather." Daddy stomped down the stairs and past me out the front door. "Call Grandma Hughes if you have an emergency!" Mom added, following him.

I ran out onto the porch. "What's going on?"

No answers.

"Is Maria all right?"

Mom slammed the door shut and then rolled down her window. "I can't go into it right now, Liz. You'll find out soon enough."

Mom's words were an understatement. I woke about six-thirty in the morning to hear Daddy yelling and Maria crying. It was the most disgusting conversation I'd ever heard in my life.

"Let's hear all about it, Maria," he said, his voice dripping with sarcastic sympathy. "I want *all* the details. I'm not sure I understand."

Maria was sobbing. "I don't want to tell you again."

"Well, that's too bad, Gilly-monster, because I intend to find out just what kind of daughter I've raised."

Daddy taunted her about sleeping with a married man, the supervisor where she was working. One minute he was yelling at her, condemning her in the harshest tones; the next minute he was pumping her in a vile way for emotional and mechanical details.

"I didn't seduce him! He came on to me first!" Fifteen-year-old Maria finally stood up in her own defense.

Daddy knew he was getting to her then, and he didn't hesitate to say things that would hurt even worse.

"No, no. That's not true," Maria sobbed. "You're full of lies. Jason loves me. I know he does."

Mom spoke up suddenly. It was the first time she had ever interfered on our behalf. "That's enough, Chuck. We've listened to you for hours. We'd all like to get some sleep."

"I'll decide when this is over," Daddy said.

"No!" Mom screamed. "I said it's over, and it *is* over. Maria, get to bed. Chuck, you can keep your mouth shut or go back to Texas. I've had enough. I don't want to hear you say anything about this subject ever again."

Daddy was furious. "I warned you about guys and hormones, Maria. But you wouldn't believe me, would you? Well, how does it feel to be used goods?"

"Chuck!" Mom shrieked.

Daddy stormed out the back door, muttering loudly, "Like mother, like daughter—apparently it runs in the family."

/ / / 20 / / /

I was standing outside one searing July afternoon, watching the twins ride their new bicycles around the backyard. Practice was making them so good that the neighborhood would never be the same again. Then the phone rang, and I ran inside to answer it.

"Hello. Hughes residence."

"Hi, Liz. This is Darren."

"Hi, Darren!" My stomach did an elated flip-flop, but I managed to keep my voice cool as I asked, "What's up?"

"Not much. I have tickets to the Gila Ranch Hayride tomorrow night. Wanna' go?"

"Sure, I'd love to go with you. I haven't been on a hayride since I was a little kid."

"Really? My whole family goes every year."

My mind was clicking. *Whole family?* I thought.

"My sisters and their kids will be coming with us, too. It's a big group, and we always have a blast."

What could I wear that would impress his whole family? What would happen if he wanted to meet *my* family? "Yes, Darren. I . . . . I'd love to meet your family. That'll be great."

"Okay," he said, sounding glad I'd accepted. "I'll pick you up about six-thirty. Oh, and come hungry," he added. "They have great barbecued ribs."

As soon as we'd said good-bye, I raised my fist to the sky,

screeching with delight. "Yes. Yes! *Yes!*" I spun around and jogged down the hallway. Then I ran back to the phone and called Teri to share the news as fast as my mouth could move.

Our first date was wonderful. Darren's family was happy and friendly—very much, I supposed, like the television family of my dreams. His father was a calm, reverent man. His mother was gracious and welcoming. His brother and two sisters were there to have fun—and did we ever!

But I probably enjoyed myself more than anyone else. Somehow, I'd managed to land in the situation of my dreams. Now that this guy had bitten my hook, I wanted desperately to reel him in. The surprising thing was that over the weeks that followed, the fish reeled me in.

No matter how hard I tried to hide my family's troubles from Darren, they always seemed to seep out at the edges. Unlike my other friends, male or female, he didn't walk away. He witnessed the tension, the anger, and the misery, and he kept coming back to me.

Maria and I were alone with the twins one weeknight, when Daddy arrived home unexpectedly. "Where's your mother?" he demanded.

"I dunno," Maria answered.

Daddy's face was turning red, so I added, "She said she had to run some errands."

The red got darker. "The same kind of errands she's been busy with for the last couple of months?" he asked, as if it were our fault. "Well, let's just see who she's with this week."

Maria and I spent the next hour worrying ourselves sick. We had no idea which bar Mom had gone to, so we couldn't warn her. What if Daddy went looking for her and she was dancing with another man? "He'd kill the guy," Maria whispered, "and then Mom, for sure." Finally, we put the twins to bed and began preparing to weather a very large storm by going to bed early, too.

We didn't have to wait long. "You're a disgrace to this family!" Daddy yelled as the front door banged open.

Mom was apparently ignoring all the obscenities he was

shouting. We heard her climb the stairs, go into the bedroom, hang up her clothes, and climb into bed. Her attitude was making Daddy furious.

"Don't you have anything to say for yourself?" he growled.

"No, I don't, Chuck." Mom's voice was emotionless. "To be honest, I don't care how you feel or what you think. I'm through centering my life on the most selfish and inconsiderate man I've ever met. I'm through kissing your feet."

Maria and I crawled out of bed and over to our door, knowing that Daddy was really going to lose control. Crouching in the darkness, we waited anxiously.

Sure enough. He was lost in red anger. "That's just fine, Maureen, because I don't plan on spending another day married to a slut!" We heard Daddy scoop Mom up, and we followed at a distance as he stomped down the stairs and through the kitchen to the back door. He threw her out, and she hit hard. But Mom knew Daddy wasn't through. She jumped up and took off running in her pajamas.

"You keep your hands off my mother, you big fat jerk!" I screamed, sprinting across the kitchen.

Daddy swirled around and punched me squarely in the face. I went flying into a plate-glass window. "Mind your own business if you want to see tomorrow," he growled as he bolted out the back door.

When I heard the glass shatter around me, suddenly I realized that what had just occurred was identical to the dream that had been awakening me for so many nights—but this time it was real. I was living it.

Maria hurried to see if I was okay. I had a few nasty cuts, but miraculously, most of the broken glass had fallen onto the patio outside, and I had landed inside on the kitchen floor. "Listen," I told her, struggling to clear my head, "we've *got* to get help!"

Slipping jeans under our nightgowns, we ran to the intersection and flagged down a policeman. Within moments, one officer was on the front porch while another canvassed the neighborhood. Sister Benson heard all the commotion and took us into her home.

We'd been sitting there a while when I suddenly had a terrifying thought. Charlie and Vaughn were alone! Grabbing Maria, I ran out the door, only to discover the policeman talking with Daddy on the porch. Daddy had one of the twins under each arm. He saw Maria and me coming as he walked across the front lawn. "If you want your mother, you can have her," he shouted, "but I'm taking my kids away. Look close. You'll never see them again!"

/ / / / /

"Things were really bad at Liz's house by the time I came into the picture," Darren said quietly, somewhat changing the subject.

"You called it the blackest hole, the deepest pit of your life," Ben said to me. "How was the Holy Ghost still with you?"

Now I had to think. That part of my life had been so dark and full of screaming tension. "The inner voice was there," I began slowly. "The voice was there, but fear and anxiety and alcohol made it downright impossible for me to hear the whispers. I forgot to listen. Then a funny thing happened. I don't know for a fact that it was the Holy Ghost, but I feel very sure it was."

"The dreams?" Darren broke in.

"Yes, I began having dreams—nightmares, really. In them, I lived out horrible situations, like the night Daddy threw Mom out the door and then punched me. That was when I realized I was living the nightmares I'd been having. I didn't know what to do about my premonitions being fulfilled, but it happened many, many times."

"So you're saying that those premonitory dreams were messages from the Holy Ghost?" Ben looked surprised.

"No," I answered, but then I reconsidered. "Well, yes, maybe. The idea never occurred to me then. But I can see now that I never calmed down enough to listen to the Spirit. It's only been in the last few years that Darren and I have talked about those dreams and wondered if they weren't a sort of confirmation.

They're proof to me that even though I felt abandoned, I was never entirely alone."

Darren added, "The Holy Ghost can speak in a lot of ways. He teaches and prompts and comforts. And He can chastise and confirm things, too. When we thought about it prayerfully, Liz and I were able to identify most of those influences in her life. I think everyone can."

/ / / / /

Perhaps watching my nightmare become reality was the reason I felt something impending the night the twins were stolen. When Daddy said we'd never see them again, fear slammed at my stomach. "How could we have been so stupid?" I moaned, sinking to the ground and crying.

As soon as Daddy drove away, Mom crawled out of the bushes around the library down the street. Maria and I sat on the grass crying while she answered the officers' questions.

"It'll be okay," Mom announced, pulling us to our feet and walking into the house. "No judge in this state will let that man keep your brother and sister. He has a pretty impressive police record."

"You never signed the papers," I said between tears.

"Yes, but the record for reports of domestic violence is there because of all the times you girls have called the cops."

Mom was right—the twins were returned. But that was when Daddy gave new meaning to violence. He broke into our home on several occasions, called continually at late hours, followed Mom when she went places, and tried to kidnap Charlie and Vaughn from their day-care center. He even cut the brake line on Mom's car.

Fortunately, she wasn't hurt. But one day, not long after that, she told Maria and me that we needed to talk. "Daddy has started seeing a marriage counselor," Mom explained.

Maria made a scoffing sound.

"He says he wants to show good faith and prove that he truly does want to change. But the counselor called me today and warned us that your dad is a very dangerous person. We're not to believe a thing he says. Not one thing! The counselor warned that he will do anything to fool us into taking him back."

"He's sick," I commented, in what was likely the biggest understatement of the year.

"Do *not* trust him—ever. Do you understand?"

Maria and I told her we did. But during the months that followed, we were surprised by the new lengths Daddy went to for attention. He began threatening suicide at least twice a week. Again, the counselor phoned and told us not to believe a word Dad said. I had no trouble following the counselor's advice—the voice inside me agreed one hundred percent.

But there was one message the Spirit was whispering that I absolutely refused to hear. It said that Darren and I were spending too much time alone together. He came to my school functions, we went to church dances and firesides, and even when I had to baby-sit, Darren hung around.

One night, as we arrived back at my house after the homecoming dance, Darren's headlights illuminated someone breaking into our back door. Daddy! Mom had put double locks on all of the doors, so it took a key to get through them no matter which way a person was going. But there Daddy was, trying to jimmy the lock.

Without a second thought, I ran to the Bensons' to phone the police. We had a protective order, and it was illegal for Daddy to come within five miles of our house.

Using his Chevy Luv pickup, Darren tried to block the driveway and box Daddy in while I made the call. But Daddy ran wildly for his Trans Am and revved the engine. You'd have thought he was a movie stuntman, the way he drove across the lawn, flew out over the gutter, and sped off down the road.

If any guy was going to be deterred from a girl, that ought to have done it. I expected Darren to back off. But he didn't. He seemed surprised by my loony father and strained family relations, but apparently he didn't think they reflected poorly on me. And when it came down to faults of my own, I could see that he cared deeply. Instead of using name-calling or hitting or temper tantrums, he spoke calmly with me. I was amazed to discover that people could talk about their disappointments, condemn something wrong, and still be filled with love.

My drinking, for example. On the day of Darren's first football game, I desperately wanted to relax, to forget, to have a good time. So I guzzled until I was sloshed. When Darren found out, it was obvious that he didn't approve. I fully expected him to go away. Instead, he put his hand on my cheek, causing me to look him squarely in the eye.

"Liz," he said, "this behavior is disgusting." Disappointment and hurt filled his eyes, but so did love. That was when I knew he really cared about me.

After that, with Darren's help, I learned to stay sober. We continued growing closer and closer. And yes, I realized we were getting pretty intimate with one another, but I didn't pay any attention to thoughts that it might have been wrong. When I was with Darren, I felt appreciated. He knew my weaknesses and my family's troubles, but he loved me anyway. Giving him all my love in return seemed a natural, beautiful thing to do.

/ / / 21 / / / /

Late one rainy evening, the night before Easter, Darren and I arrived home from a swing-choir performance. Because of the way Mom had set up the new locks on our house, we had to wait on the porch for someone to let us in.

When she swung the door open, Maria screamed. "There's a light on in the garage!"

Darren and I turned to look. Through the window on the side of the garage, we could see the dome light of Daddy's Trans Am. I couldn't see Daddy anywhere, "How'd he get in there?"

"Go turn the patio light on, Liz," Darren shouted.

I flipped the switch and ran back down the steps. Meanwhile, Darren was dragging Daddy through the garage door and onto the driveway. "Tell your mom to phone an ambulance," he commanded.

The house was in an uproar. "Mom, call 911! We need an ambulance! It's Daddy—he's—"

The next thing I knew, I was kneeling at Daddy's side. Darren was administering mouth-to-mouth resuscitation.

"Darren," I said, pressing Daddy's wrist in my hand, "I can't find a pulse."

Darren just kept breathing into Daddy's mouth and pushing on his chest.

"I can't find a pulse!"

Darren's rhythm didn't break.

Within seconds, we were surrounded by flashing red lights. Neighbors were gathering along the perimeter of our rain-soaked yard. Distantly, as if it were a hundred miles away, I saw Sister Benson take Maria and the twins. The men in the ambulance relieved Darren, and Mom ran to get her purse for the trip to the hospital.

"It's a DOA," the paramedic said, just after she'd gone.

I knew I'd heard that abbreviation before, but I couldn't bring the meaning of it to the surface of my mind. Then, as I stood watching, the paramedics heaved Daddy's body onto a gurney. They covered his face with a sheet.

"He's dead?" I gasped, looking up at Darren.

Darren nodded. Like pillars of stone, we stood watching them load Daddy's body into the ambulance.

Mom ran up, breathless. "Liz," she grabbed my arm. "You take care of things—Aunt Irene's on her way over—and I'll call as soon as I have any word on his condition."

"Ma'am?" A police officer interrupted. "Do you have a suicide note?"

"What?" Mom was pale and shocked.

"Did he leave a note?"

"A note? I don't know. Why?"

"If he didn't leave a note, we'll be needing a signature right here," the officer said, holding up a clipboard and a pen, "to perform an autopsy. Then we'll be able to determine the cause of death."

"Death?" Mom said, one hand flying up to her forehead. "He's dead?"

Chagrined, the officer realized she hadn't known. "Yes, ma'am," he said more tenderly. "I'm terribly sorry."

"Dear God!" my mother screamed, collapsing in a heap. "He's dead and still hurting me. Dead . . . dead . . . " she began crying, her small body racked with heaving sobs. "Please, God. Please, someone—anyone! Please make him stop!"

The paramedics quickly surrounded Mom. Her sister, Irene, drove up only moments later, and they half-lifted her into Irene's car. Soon everyone had driven away into the night. Darren and I were left alone in the dark, wet driveway.

When Darren put his arms around me, I melted into hot tears. "That jerk!" I cried. "That horrible, awful jerk! How could he do this to Mom? What about the twins, now? That selfish, selfish jerk!"

Darren led me into the house and sat me on the sofa. Then he ran for the bathroom. Over my own sobbing, I could hear him throwing up again and again. He'd breathed in a lot of carbon monoxide while doing mouth-to-mouth.

When he came out a few minutes later, he was trying not to show how affected he was by the whole ordeal. "Liz," he said, kneeling on the floor by my feet.

I coughed against the hiccoughing sobs I couldn't seem to control, and looked into his face.

"I swear to you, Liz," he spoke with earnest intensity. "No one will ever hurt you again, Liz. I will not let it happen." Then Darren put his arms around me. "I love you," he said, kissing me gently.

/ / / / /

My cheeks were wet again, but I was seated in a bishop's office, not standing in the dark, empty driveway. Just remembering that night ripped open my heart.

"Love came into my life the night Daddy left. Someone really, truly loved me in a selfless way, and I loved him, too."

Darren cleared his throat a little uncomfortably, but I wanted very much for Ben to understand the healing power of love.

"There were times when I treated him spitefully, when I didn't know how to trust, when I was afraid. And sometimes he got fed up, too. But he never quit loving me. He just went on. I think it was the unconditional nature of his love that finally won through. That, and my own desire to become a whole enough person that I could return his love the same way. For a long time I enjoyed receiving it, but I didn't really know how to feel those positive emotions anymore. Anger and sadness were the only things I knew how to feel."

When I stopped talking, the room was still once more, but at last Ben asked, "Your father is dead?"

I nodded.

"And was it all over when he left your life?"

Was it over? I laughed a little. There were times when I felt that it would never be over.

/ / / / /

Bishop Randolph and his counselors came to our home the day before the funeral to assist Mom with the last few details. The house was very quiet except for their low voices. Suddenly, Mom's voice shot out, sharp and loud. "He will, and that's final!"

The men gave soft-spoken explanations, followed by Mom's angry answer, "You're not the judge. If he'd had a choice, Chuck would have wanted to be buried in his temple clothes. If God decides he's not worthy, then *He* can remove the clothing!"

Fuming, Mom showed the three men out. "It's a good thing he's a brand-new bishop. I'll overlook his arrogance," she muttered. Then, seeing me watching from the next room, she asked, "What are you staring at?"

I was looking at my mother. I was trying to understand what had become of her. Silently, I opened my American history book and started reading again.

The funeral was held during the week of Easter break— Easter! A time of new beginnings, a time when people celebrate Christ's sacrifice and resurrection. I thought back over all the changes in my life since Easter a year before: I'd turned sixteen, Daddy had finally graduated, our family had blown apart entirely, I'd met Darren . . . and now I was free!

Lots of people came to Daddy's funeral, and the service was a well-done memorial. It was an emotional group. People cried openly through it, but I showed nothing.

My emotions were very different from those of most of the mourners. I was angry on behalf of my mom—angry for what she'd become because of that man. I also felt an overwhelming sense of relief. No one would be hitting me for trumped-up reasons, ruling my life like a tyrant, standing at the foot of my bed in the middle of the night, or trying to put his hands where I didn't want them. Darren was right: no one would ever hurt me again. Daddy could control me no longer.

Grandpa Hughes took me aside between the funeral and the graveside services. "You were real cold in there, Liz. Someday you are going to hate what you've done."

I looked at Grandpa Hughes in silent surprise. Hate what *I'd* done? *I* didn't beat, abuse, or attack. I certainly didn't kill that horrible man.

"Your dad really loved you girls. He took care of you when no one else would. Someday you're going to wake up and realize how very much you hurt him. I hope you can live with the guilt," my grandfather said pointedly, turning and walking away into the continuing wet drizzle.

I was speechless. How many other people thought it was my fault—Mom's and Maria's and mine? Apparently Daddy's family did. Who else?

Darren slipped his arm around my shoulder. "Is everything okay?"

"Just hold me tight," I pleaded, curling into his embrace.

From the safety of that spot, I reviewed the situation. Darren had become a deliverer for me. During the past several months, he'd rescued my mother and sister and me from potentially dangerous situations. He'd helped me give up the bottle and was even after me now to quit drinking caffeinated sodas. He thought far more of me than I did of myself. For example, he always said I had strength and faith he admired—even when I didn't think I had any faith left.

Because of these things, and many others, I knew he genuinely cared. His love was like gentle sunshine that kept a tiny part of my heart warm and alive. I responded to his goodness.

Watching my mom had plainly shown me what living in fear and anger could do to a person. As she became more and more distant, Mom also grew into a person whose misery spread around her like a cloud. Constantly expressing guilt, she would say she ought to have done this or that. Then she'd place blame:

you kids should have tried harder; you were the center of most of our arguments.

I wanted to escape again. Why couldn't the nightmare end? It just kept dragging on and on. . . .

/   /   /   /   /

"No, Ben," I said, noticing the gleam in his eye. "You know very well it wasn't over. That's when my life really began."

Ben crossed his legs, one ankle resting on the other knee, spread his notebook open across his lap, and leaned back in a go-ahead gesture.

"Up to this point, the abuse had happened *to* me. But once I escaped my father, *I chose* to make things happen."

"I've known you long enough to know you're something of a spitfire," Ben chuckled. "I can't imagine you not stirring things up!"

"You've got me there," I grinned. "But the girl I was at seventeen is not the same person sitting here now."

Darren whistled teasingly, but I ignored him.

"One day, in a cold, high-school bathroom, vomiting my guts out, I gave up on life. After that, it seemed my emotions were dead—or at least, certain ones seemed to have been lost to me."

"Go on," Ben prodded when I paused.

"Anger, fear, pain, sadness, shame—these were feelings that had become my companions. I was more comfortable with them than I was with joy or love, because I wasn't used to positive emotions anymore. I didn't trust them."

"What attracted you to this cynical teenager?" Ben asked Darren, only half-teasingly.

I didn't give my husband a chance to answer. "People liked my dad when they didn't know his other side. I learned hypocrisy from a master," I explained. "I knew how to make others laugh and relax, have a good time, break all the rules and think it was fun. Besides, I quit letting myself get very close to anyone—except Darren."

"But you trusted him?"

"Yes and no," I answered, taking a deep breath. "He never

gave me any reason not to trust him. He just loved me in spite of everything I was ashamed of. At first, I suppose I didn't love him in a healthy way. But I was drawn to him, and I gave him the kind of love I knew. Granted, my love was full of shallow counterfeits and mistakes, but I recognized that his love was what I needed. I was approaching it from the only angle I'd ever known."

/ / / 22 / / /

Mom," I said, walking into her bedroom while she was getting ready to take off on another weekend of partying with her new boyfriend, "I need to talk to you."

"Make it quick, Liz," she answered, putting on a pair of turquoise earrings. "I don't want to be late."

"Okay, you asked for it! Darren and I are engaged, Mom. We're expecting a baby in about seven months." Putting my news so bluntly would be sure to knock her socks off.

Mom didn't even flinch. "I know," she remarked casually, painting on her lipstick. When she finished, she blotted the excess on a tissue and added, "We'll talk Monday. Okay?"

I stared at her. "What do you mean, 'I know'?"

"You've been looking very pale lately, Liz," she said, fluffing the pillows on her bed and making sure everything in her room was straight. "All your life you've had a phenomenal amount of energy—until the past few weeks. Now you've got dark circles that are almost as green as your eyes are! And that red hair of yours has lost its color and shine. You look like something the cat dragged in. Besides, seeing how you're always with Darren . . . well, it doesn't take a rocket scientist to figure out two plus two." Snatching up her purse, she said, "Gotta go, or I'll be late. Oh," she stuck her head back in the bedroom door. "I still love ya."

Mom stayed away all weekend and went off again the next

weekend, too, as was becoming her routine. Darren, according to our habit, came over while I ran the fort.

It was a beautiful evening in early summer. A cool breeze whispered through the orange trees surrounding our patio and sent a spray of spent blossoms swirling gently onto the tiles. The leaves of the eucalyptus tree Daddy had planted behind his toolshed made a soft rustling sound. And the brilliant pinks and purples of the Arizona sunset painted the sky and then faded gently into twilight. Maria went to a movie, and Darren put the twins to bed because I wasn't feeling at all well.

"This is normal," Darren said comfortingly. "Women always throw up when they're pregnant."

"But they don't have cramps," I moaned, holding my stomach.

As the beautiful twilight gave way to darkness and the hours of night crawled by, I became very ill. Finally, about three or four in the morning, I slept.

Darren's dad was waiting for him when he returned home. "I don't believe you two are married yet," he observed when Darren staggered in at dawn.

"You're right," Darren answered, blurting it all out. "Liz was really sick tonight. We think she had the flu, and we were concerned—she's pregnant, you see, and we're engaged." He'd been wondering how to break the news. Now it was done.

Darren's father stood silent for several moments, realizing that the time for teaching gospel principles in theory was past. His son had already enrolled in the school of hard knocks. "When the tune is done," Darren's dad said softly, patting his son on the back, "someone has to pay the fiddler."

The wedding hall looked like a bowery of flowers. Brother Benson walked me down the aisle and gave me away, placing my hand on Darren's arm.

But in the midst of all the flowers and smiles and traditions, Bishop Randolph's preliminary remarks were simply to the point. Without apology, he extended a goal for Darren and me to get our lives in order and go to the temple. He admonished us to be sealed to each other for eternity, and then he performed a brief ceremony that made us husband and wife for time.

Rude, I thought. *On my special day, he tries to hold something over my head!* Going to the temple was of no interest to me. I had no intention of going through what my mother had endured. From that moment on, the bishop's words fell on deaf ears and a heart of stone.

/ / / / /

Ben shut his notebook and placed his scriptures on top, spreading them open where his notes had been. "Are you familiar with Jacob 2:31–35?" he asked.

"Is that the scripture about women and children whose hearts have died?" Darren asked. Ben nodded as he searched for the page.

"A friend of mine calls that being soul-murdered," I said. "It's when you can't feel positive emotions like love and joy anymore. Those are the things that feed your spirit, so without them you become a hardened, burnt-out shell."

"Exactly," Ben smiled. "Jacob put it this way: 'I, the Lord, have seen the sorrow, and heard the mourning of the daughters of my people. . . . Ye have broken the hearts of your tender wives, . . . and the sobbings of their hearts ascend up to God against you.' Then," he nodded at Darren, "the part you're referring to, 'many hearts died, pierced with deep wounds.' "

"Doesn't it say right in there that God will not suffer the cries of those fair daughters to come up to Him against the men?" Darren asked. "I'm pretty sure it goes so far as to say they cannot lead those daughters away into captivity because of their tenderness, without the Lord cursing them—even unto destruction."

"That's it, in a nutshell!" Ben grinned. "So I suppose you've already noticed what led me to this scripture. In this chapter, Jacob is calling the Nephite men of his day to repentance for unchastity. But I have long thought that it seems to apply very specifically to the problems we've been talking about, too."

"Like the hearts that died, pierced with deep wounds?" I asked, thinking of my mother and Maria and myself.

"Exactly," Ben answered, closing his Book of Mormon and zipping it shut. "Elizabeth, what can you tell me about healing a broken heart—a heart that's been, as you say, 'soul-murdered'?"

I thought about this question for some time, while the men waited quietly. I thought of many things: of the healing power in love, of the importance of the wounded person wanting to let go of the pain and to be willing to be healed, and of how doing that requires humility and faith.

"I can't imagine there's a single easy sentence that answers your question," I began hesitantly. "But I'm sure of one thing. Nothing short of the atonement of Jesus Christ can heal such a wound. It is important for priesthood leaders to help in cleansing it, for loving friends and even therapists to bind it. But then, only the healing power of the Master Physician can actually resurrect tissues that have died. Christ is the only one who can cause them to knit together again and function once more."

This was the deepest core of my testimony. There were no words to express the depth of my feelings about the Savior's love or the power He wants to exercise on our behalf.

"Perhaps the greatest realization of my life—the key to healing for me—came when I suddenly understood that Christ saves us not only from our sins but also from our afflictions, our sorrows, and our inabilities. The Atonement doesn't apply just to the mistakes Darren and I made before we were married, or to the hatred I felt as a child, or to any other chain that has ever bound us. The Lord knelt in Gethsemane so that He might provide a way whereby I could break the chains that have bound my family for generations."

I was crying again, but this time the tears grew from the depth of my gratitude. "Do you see?" I asked. "Do you understand? The Atonement was made to save me from my pain. That's what eternal life is all about. My Savior wants me to have eternal joy."

Silence again bound us together. When I reached toward

Ben's scriptures, he handed them to me. Opening the Bible to Isaiah 61, I read the words of the Messiah. "I have come, he said, 'to preach good tidings unto the meek; . . . to bind up the brokenhearted, to proclaim liberty to the captives, and the opening of the prison to them that are bound: . . . to comfort all that mourn; . . . to give unto them beauty for ashes, the oil of joy for mourning, the garment of praise for the spirit of heaviness.' "

"Christ is the Ultimate Physician," I said. "He's the one who can resurrect a murdered soul and give that soul what it takes to be a chainbreaker. He's the only one."

Quiet lay between us once more. At last Ben spoke softly. "I see. But how does it happen? From your experience, what brought the Lord's hand into your life?"

Ben's questions were so hard. I thought of myself at the time of my wedding. By my own actions, I'd pretty much closed my ears to the whispering of that inner voice. I trusted almost no one, and my emotions had—in many ways—become hard.

"Time has been a good friend," I answered. "Over time I have been able to draw upon the grace of Christ by using the tools available to me. And to do that . . . well, I already pointed out how making the Atonement meaningful in our lives requires humility and faith."

"That's a big demand for someone who's lost in feelings of shame and distrust," Ben observed.

"Believe me, I know!" I answered. "But I didn't say how much of those qualities we need. All I said was that we have to do our best—whatever it may be—to exercise faith and humility. Everyone falls short of the mark—that's why a Savior was provided. He said, 'My grace is sufficient for all men that humble themselves before me.'[1] That means, once we do everything we can, Christ's grace takes over through the Atonement."

Wisely, Darren added, "With time."

/ / / / /

After our reception, Darren and I spent our honeymoon at a little cabin overlooking the Grand Canyon. From our doorstep we watched the varied colors of the desert, the myriad changing hues within the depths of that vast gorge.

On the second night I woke up screaming from one of my usual nightmares.

"Liz?" Darren had his arms tight around me. "Liz! Are you all right?"

"Uh, yeah, sure," I answered shakily. "Just a dream."

Darren began stroking my hair. "A dream? What could be that bad?"

"I . . . I don't remember," I lied. Crawling out of bed, I started toward the bathroom for a drink of water. "It must have been a pretty intense one, though. I'm still shaking!" I said, laughing.

Once in the bathroom, I glared into the dark mirror and bit back tears. Even after I'd finally gotten away from my father, away from my home and into the arms of someone kind and good, my past was still haunting me. The dream was still clear in my mind—every stark, vivid detail. The groping hands and peering eyes that I forced out of my thoughts each day had come, as always, to clutch at me in the night.

I couldn't tell Darren the darkest secret of all. I was sure that if I did—if Darren really knew me—it would mean the loss of the best thing I'd ever had.

NOTE

1. Ether 12:27.

/ / / 23 / / /

One month after we were married, Darren and I loaded up his battered Chevy Luv pickup and hitched a small U-haul trailer to the back. We were heading out into the big, vast world, where Darren had been accepted for admission to a university in Saint Paul, Minnesota.

As we were giving our last hugs through the windows and pulling away from the curb, Darren's dad handed him a roll of quarters. "I want a phone call every night until you're settled," he told Darren. Then, with gruffness that revealed the depth of his emotion, he added, "I don't want your mother worrying herself sick."

Darren promised he'd call, waving one last time to his mom, and we were off.

The future seemed a blossom of promise, like a delicate desert flower growing out of a dry, brittle bush. My heart raced whenever I thought about how soon I would be a mother. And at the same time, I assured myself that I would finish my senior year of high school right on schedule.

But if our future together was a lovely, unfolding flower, it soon became apparent that the stem had sprouted a sharp, persistent thorn. I was keeping a secret hidden—a dark memory that waited each night to prick me.

/ / / / /

"Liz! Wake up!" Darren's voice was caring, but a hint of exasperation hung about the edges as he turned on the lamp and pulled me into his arms. "It's another nightmare, Liz. That's all. Just another of your nightmares."

I'd married a good man and traveled far away from my childhood, yet Daddy's abuse still had me shackled in chains of steel. Each link had a character of its own, and two of the heaviest were anger and fear. Fear was clenching tight around me that night, overflowing even into my feelings toward my husband. Yet, though I was trembling, I clung to him.

"Look, Liz," he said with firm gentleness, "I know your relationship with your dad is behind these bad dreams. I know he hurt you terribly, but he's gone now. Chuck can't hurt you anymore."

Although Darren rubbed my shoulders soothingly, I wasn't able to calm down. I kept thinking Daddy was at the foot of my bed. Night after night, I'd been dreaming that when I woke up he'd be standing there. I was tired of being constantly shadowed by fear. While I slept, it lurked in the darkness just beyond my feet; while I was awake, it shadowed my thoughts. And during intimate moments it drove me to irrational misery.

Completely innocent, Darren would unwittingly say some of the same things my father had said to me, and those trigger words sent me vaulting into the past. I became a child again, alone, a victim.

At last, when he could see that I was beyond comfort, Darren's patience wore thin. Frustrated and confused by the invisible chains that bound me, he repeated, "Chuck can't hurt you anymore, Liz. He's in God's hands now." Then he reached over to the nightstand and turned through the pages of his seminary Bible. "Remember that scripture we read the other day? Here it is—Matthew 18, verse 6: 'But whoso shall offend one of these little ones which believe in me, it were better for him that a millstone were hanged about his neck, and that he were drowned in the depth of the sea.' "

Darren said, "You are one of those 'little ones,' Liz." Then he put his arms around me again. "Believe in Him, and let it go."

"Oh, Darren!" I shouted, crying and pushing him away. "You

don't understand. I share some of the guilt! God would never have allowed such terrible things to happen unless He was angry with me. God won't let me forget those things." I felt my chest heave as I drew a deep, furious breath. Spitefully I muttered, "And if Daddy is in what you call 'spirit prison,' he and Satan certainly aren't letting me forget, either!"

Darren stared at me, exhausted and utterly confused.

I glared back at him for one long, painful moment, wishing there was something one of us could do. Then I dropped my face into my hands and sobbed with anger and fear.

"Liz," he said at last, working to remain tender and calm. "What on earth are you talking about? God doesn't punish people that way."

I could do nothing but weep.

"God disapproves of physical violence," he said.

"Oh, Darren," I moaned, rocking back and forth with grief that I thought would somehow tear me wide open. "Oh, if only it had just been physical!"

"Well, I know there was emotional abuse, too . . . " he faltered.

I looked up at him through my fingers. His mouth had shut hard, and his eyes had grown very serious.

Something inside my heart said to tell him, that now was the time. But my mind screamed at me to stop! Divulging my secret would destroy my marriage, I reasoned. He wouldn't want me when he knew the truth. *Tell him,* my heart urged. *He'll try to understand. It isn't fair this way.*

I bit my lip and worked at getting myself under control. Cautiously, I considered what things I could tell. *Tell all,* my heart prodded. And so, slowly, I began to divulge even the ugliest details.

Darren sat like a silent pillar in the bed, horrified by what I was trying to say. The longer he sat motionless, the more desperately I struggled to make him understand.

"Enough!" he suddenly shouted. Fuming, he leaped up from the bed and began pacing the floor. Fear jerked through my insides as I wondered if he was going to vent his anger on me.

I was always looking for a second face—always suspecting that he had one, always waiting to see it come forward.

But the fury was never cast in my direction, not even now. At last he strode to his nightstand and grabbed his scriptures again, this time the Doctrine and Covenants. I watched, curious, as he stormed through the pages. He stood motionless by the lamp, reading in the same spot for a very long time.

Days later, he told me that a fire had been burning inside him, demanding revenge. When he prayed mentally for help against the consuming anger, the passage in Doctrine and Covenants 98:23–24 had come into his mind, and he'd read it over again and again until the flames finally came under his control: "Now, I speak unto you concerning your families," the scripture began, "if men will smite you, or your families, once, and ye bear it patiently and revile not against them, neither seek revenge, ye shall be rewarded; but if ye bear it not patiently, it shall be accounted unto you as being meted out as a just measure unto you."[1]

All at once, as if he had suddenly remembered I was there, Darren looked toward where I sat huddled beneath the bedding. "I love you, Liz," he whispered, sitting down beside me and curling his arms around me.

We stayed that way for a long, long time, and at last I slipped again into sleep. Afterward I learned that Darren had remained awake through the night, alone with his agonizing thoughts.

/ / / / /

"Time is also an important tool the Savior uses in healing," Darren said. "Surely, as a physician, you see proof of that every day."

"Absolutely." Ben nodded in agreement. "I see it in the healing of both physical and spiritual wounds." He drew a deep breath as if to ask something, but then, apparently thinking better of it, he paused.

"Go on," Darren urged. "Ask."

"Well," Ben began, "it has been my experience that spouses are also victimized by the perpetrator's sexual abuse. What I was wondering about was the significance of your comment on time. I assume you based it on your own, personal ordeal."

"That's perceptive of you," Darren said with a hint of surprise in his voice. Then, after some thought, he added, "You know, at first I was shocked by the vehemence of my own anger and internal demand for revenge. I endured many strong, consuming feelings, and I wasn't sure if I was justified in having them."

Ben nodded.

"But Liz and I have discussed my feelings at length, as well as hers. With time, we've come to understand that these reactions are natural."

Darren gently reached out and took my hand into his. I knew that reassuring love grip well; he wanted me to listen carefully to what he was saying and understand what he really meant beyond the words.

"When a man discovers that the woman he married has been abused, he feels as though their relationship has been violated—*he* has been violated. He may feel that this marvelous, choice woman whom he chose above all others suddenly seems tarnished, much as if you turned over a beautiful piece of silver and found the back had oxidized and discolored. The value of that silver is *no less*. But a husband's first instinct is to rub off the stain. Then he realizes it's not a stain but a scar."

Ben smiled. "Scars aren't easily removed."

"Exactly!" Darren returned the smile of understanding. "I was powerless to reach out and instantly make Liz better. I felt hurt—even cheated. The most sacred, intimate, private part of our relationship was haunted by a ghost from her past. My own ego began to suffer as well."

"And so what did you do?" Ben prodded.

"That's the point—there seemed to be nothing I could do. I was the protector of my family, yet my hands were tied. Only Liz could determine whether she was going to be made well. No matter how I agonized, I could not erase my wife's pain."

Darren let my hand go and shifted in his chair. "I didn't stop trying to help her, though," he said. He stood up and took a few steps back and forth across the room. "Ben, I felt like a blind surgeon performing an excruciating, delicate surgery on the person I loved most in this world. The operation went on for days and then dragged into months, even years. I felt untrained and unprepared, but I discovered the tools were there before me. In time I learned how to let the Spirit be my guide."

"Tools again," Ben said. "Name them."

"They're the same ones Liz has been talking about," Darren answered, sitting back down. "Accepting the Atonement was vital for both of us. That's a tool, and so are the scriptures. They provide a powerful way for an abused person to begin to replant trust in his or her heart. Prayer is another tool. It's the source through which you can invite divine intervention to enter the healing process. Turning away from revenge and focusing on what we could control was an important part of changing our attitude, too."

"That's right," I broke in. "Attitude is a tool we discovered was within our control. For example, the attitude we took toward gratitude made a difference. Expressing gratitude for every little thing that was right in our lives was like planting little seeds of hope and faith."

Ben began counting on his fingers. "The Atonement, the guidance of the Holy Ghost, scriptures, prayer, and attitude. You also mentioned love and trust before."

"And the priesthood," Darren added. "That's a very important tool God has provided."

I'd never fully realized just how significant the priesthood was until I heard Elder Scott's conference address. When he said, "Relief comes by applying eternal truths with priesthood assistance,"[2] I realized that was true. I'd seen it in my own life. Honoring and exercising his priesthood was one of Darren's most important gifts to me.

"The priesthood," Ben added. "That's six."

"And don't forget time," Darren reminded. "Liz and I begged the Lord for a quick fix, a nice, easy solution with immediate results. But healing something like this takes time."

NOTES

1. The remaining verses of this chapter are also helpful.

2. Richard G. Scott, "Healing the Tragic Scars of Abuse," *Ensign,* May 1992, p. 31.

/ / / 24 / / /

D arren!" I screamed. "Quick! Get the nurse!"

Darren hesitated blankly for a moment. We'd been in the hospital for three days, watching women come, deliver babies, and go home. We were still trying. After thirty-six hours of hard labor, both of us were physically exhausted.

The doctors had gone into the hall to discuss a C-section, leaving Darren alone beside my bed. He looked haggard, blond stubble covering his chin and worried circles shadowing his eyes. "Liz," he said with his imperturbably careful calm, "the nurse barely left. What did you forget to ask?"

"I didn't forget anything," I bit the words out against contractions. "The baby is coming."

"She said it was still going to be a while," Darren countered, squeezing my hand. By his face I knew he was wondering if anyone understood what was going on.

"I don't care what she said!" I yelled. "She must have done something, or this baby has a mind of its own. It's coming *now!*"

Darren jumped. "We need a nurse fast!" he called, running into the hall.

The nurse walked disapprovingly into the room. "Everything's okay," she said condescendingly. "I just checked, and it's going to be a while."

Another contraction gripped me, and I shouted, "Well, I think you'd better look again!"

"Oh, my," the nurse muttered. Then she put a hand on my knee. "Whatever you do, don't push. The baby is crowning."

Within seconds the room filled with people who pushed my gurney down the hall to the delivery room. "We're not taking any chances," the doctor told me. "I'm going to use forceps. The baby's heart rate is dropping, Liz. When I say three, push with all you've got. One, two, three . . ."

Everyone cheered.

"It's a beautiful boy, Mom," the doctor said, bundling the infant up. He handed him to Darren and sent them directly down the hall to the newborn Intensive Care Unit.

By the time my husband came back, I was unconscious. Like my baby, I, too, was wheeled into intensive care. The doctor explained to Darren that I had hemorrhaged.

The first thing I remember after delivery was the pressure of blood being pumped into my arm. I looked up to see Darren kneeling beside my bed, his head bowed.

"Hi. What's going on? My arm hurts."

"Everything's fine." Darren looked up and smiled at me. "The baby is healthy, and you're going to be great."

After that I dozed back off. A nurse woke me several hours later. "Hey, Mom," she said, gently rubbing my shoulder. "It's feeding time."

My heart leaped. I was finally going to see the beautiful little boy everyone had been cooing over. As I cradled him in my arms, my heart surged with peace and warmth and love. He was precious. Blond fuzz topped his rosy complexion, and big, round eyes looked up at me. His hair was exactly the color of Darren's; I wondered if his eyes would be green like mine, when the doctor's drops wore off. It was good—so satisfying—to find both of us in him. He had all his fingers. Tears slid from my eyes as I fumbled with the blankets and accounted for all his toes as well.

"Darren," I breathed, looking up. "He's really ours! He's so tiny and . . . and perfect." Then, with a wink, I added, "When are we going to have another one?"

Darren gasped and nearly fell off his chair. He'd been beside me every minute: four long days without a rest. All he could think of now was a little sleep!

/   /   /   /   /

"Darren, you compared yourself to a surgeon, trying to bring relief to the person you love most of all," Ben said.

Darren answered, "That's right."

"And you listed the tools that were available to you."

"Yes."

"What I want to know is how you applied those tools. How did you use them?" Realizing that Darren didn't know exactly what he meant, Ben added, "Okay, say I scrubbed you up and sent you into an operating room. Perhaps you knew some of the different surgical instruments and what they were used for. But how did you go about actually performing an operation with them?"

Darren gathered his thoughts. "I suppose when you go into surgery, you don't look at the entire process as a whole. Unless I'm mistaken, you probably break it down into parts and perform them step by step. Is that right?"

"Yes."

"Remember what I said about the Holy Ghost being my guide? Well, the Holy Ghost led us just as the scriptures promise, showing 'all things what ye should do.' "[1]

"How?" Ben prodded.

Neither Darren nor I had ever tried to explain the process to someone else before, but we had talked about it together. "Okay," he said, drawing a deep breath and leaning forward in his chair. "The Atonement isn't something you can measure quantitatively. Human reasoning can't comprehend it."[2]

"Right," Ben responded.

"So experiencing it *has* to be a matter of the Spirit; it has to be shown to you by the Spirit so you can begin to comprehend it."

"I'm with you so far," Ben said.

"Well, over time, Liz and I began to discover some steps involved in healing, and I can try to outline them for you in a minute. But first, you have to understand that the element of the Spirit was vital. The Spirit taught us, cleansed us, healed us. That's why the tools of prayer and the Holy Ghost are so important. A person can follow the steps just as a physician can perform the surgery, but their success still hinges on a miracle. Just as severed tissues heal because of God's gift of life to us, so our spirits are healed only by a gift of love that we don't quite understand. We call it the Atonement."

/ / / / /

Scottie was never a very big baby. But what he didn't inherit from Darren in stature, he sure made up for in smarts. From the word *go* that child kept me busy. He began talking early and was always into something. "Grandma's revenge," Darren called it as he trundled off each Monday morning for his full load of college courses and forty-five-hour work week.

My baby was an adorable, happy companion. He almost never fussed—he kept too busy! We occupied ourselves with books and a radio, since Darren and I couldn't afford a TV.

But one morning Scottie began crying. There was apparently nothing wrong with him, but he kept fussing all day and on and on into the night. I'd tried everything: diaper changing, fresh feedings, burpings, even Numzit on the gums in case he was teething. Nothing helped.

Crying gave way to screaming. That sweet little guy just howled and howled until he was breathless. Then, as soon as he'd gasped in enough air, he'd start up again.

"Shut up!" I yelled at last, after hours without a break. "Shut up, do you hear? I can't take it anymore!"

Scottie paused for an instant at the sound of my voice and then started screaming again before I'd even finished my sentence.

"I don't know what to do for you!" I yelled. "I've tried everything."

The more I shouted at him, the louder he cried (if that was possible). As I became more upset, so did he. And the worse he got, the less control I felt. I wanted to beat that noise right out of Scottie. I raised my fist to do it—

"STOP!" I heard a loud shout, as if someone else was in the room. My hand still poised in the air, I whirled around. We were alone.

When I turned back and looked again at my son, I wondered how I could have even imagined something so hideous. Scottie was my precious, wonderful gift from God! I scooped up the screaming bundle in my arms and put him safely in his crib. Quietly, I left the room and gently closed the door.

Then I ran to the bathroom and locked myself in. I leaned against the corner and slid down the wall into a heap on the floor. It took all my willpower to pray right then. I was physically and emotionally exhausted from the hours of frustration.

"Please make him stop crying," I begged. "I can't handle this. Oh, please, Father. Tell me what to do." I pleaded with the Lord for an hour, a limp ball on the cold bathroom floor.

At last Scottie's cries began to die down, and he fell asleep. But I was terribly upset with myself. That night I realized just how effectively the chains of abuse still bound me. I felt powerless to cut myself free from a life-style of which I wanted no part. I did not want to treat my children as I'd been treated; I did not want to cope with trouble in those same violent ways. Suddenly, I no longer trusted myself. I saw myself as a time bomb, loaded years before and capable of going off at any instant.

I couldn't escape those chains; I didn't know how to make myself into the person I wanted to be. Daddy was still controlling my life! Right down to the smallest decisions—even how I would react to my own son—I was under the influence of the past.

Powerless. I felt utterly powerless against the chains. I lay there, bewildered by my own unmeasurable disappointment at not being able to trust myself.

"Liz!" Darren exclaimed, coming home and finding me alone in the bathroom, still huddled in the corner. "Are you okay?"

When he heard my story, he laughed with relief. Taking my

hand, he led me into the bedroom. "I still don't know why you're upset," he grinned. "Don't you see? You conquered your dad tonight. You took control of your emotions instead of giving in to your fury. That's victory!"

I blew my nose and didn't say a word. Apparently he didn't understand at all.

"Look, Liz," Darren said, pulling out his scriptures. "The Savior said right here in 3 Nephi 11:29, 'He that hath the spirit of contention is not of me, but is of the devil.' Just keep things in perspective. If you recognize who's trying to stir you up to anger, you're going to be fine."

I watched Darren close his scriptures. As he turned back, beaming at me, I snarled, "What planet are you from?"

Darren's smile disappeared.

"I'm disappointed in myself, and you act like everything's hunky-dory!" I stood up and shouted at him. "Your sweetness is nauseating, mister. I wanted to *beat* a baby tonight . . . *my* baby!"

Darren interrupted, "But you didn't, Liz. You should be proud of yourself."

"I'm not sure I'll be that fortunate next time," I hissed.

"Well, don't forget, you can always lock yourself in the bathroom again." Darren grinned again. "Let's take out a little insurance policy, then." He slid off the edge of the bed onto his knees, took me by the hand, and pulled me down beside him. "Let's say a prayer."

The last thing I wanted to do was pray, but I folded my arms anyway.

Darren's words were sincere and sweet. He thanked the Lord for the voice that had halted me in midswing. He begged Heavenly Father to guide and direct me. He asked that I be blessed with knowledge and patience and that my testimony might be strengthened. He implored the Lord to teach me that I was more trustworthy than I knew. And then he pleaded for my peace of mind.

I didn't understand all the things he said in the same way he did, but I appreciated his caring. Peace of mind was what I wanted more than anything else in the world. Silently I added with all the fervor of my heart, *I just want to be free of these chains, Lord. I'll do anything it takes!*

NOTES

1. 2 Nephi 32:5. Note also the emphasis on the scriptures in verse 3 and on prayer in verse 9. These tools work together.

2. Thomas S. Monson has explained: "Those who see the world only from a mortal perspective rely on human reasoning and do not claim to know that which cannot be observed, evaluated, or proven by tangible evidence. Their conclusions are only as reliable as the information available to them and their ability to evaluate it. . . . Because mankind has made such marvelous advances using only the methods of mortal perspective (logical reasoning and experimentation), some have come to rely on them exclusively. These people reject the eternal perspective because *spiritual things* (revelation, resurrection, atonement, etc.) *cannot be evaluated from a mortal perspective.*" (The Church of Jesus Christ of Latter-day Saints, "Mortal Perspective Is Limited," *Living Prophets for a Living Church,* p. 40; emphasis added.)

/ / / 25 / / /

The problem was, I didn't know what it would take to break free of my chains. I was willing to do anything, but what should I do?

With the benefit of hindsight, Darren and I have come to understand that having a sin imposed on you requires a process of healing similar to that of being forgiven of a sin. It requires the repentance process.

"You want me to list the steps for applying the tools," Darren told Ben, "and I will. But remember, although the steps are similar to those of regular repentance, I'm not suggesting that what happened to Liz was her fault. I have come to think of these steps as measures we must take to draw on the power of the Atonement."

"I'll bear that in mind," Ben said, rubbing his fingers against his beard.

"Remember being a little child in Sunday School and learning the four steps to repentance—recognizing the error, feeling remorse over it, revealing it, and making restitution for it?"

"Yes."

"Well, in the situation that was forced upon Liz, those same steps applied to her healing."

"Even though I wasn't responsible," I explained, "bad things had happened, and the smirch from someone else's decisions fell on me, too. I needed the Atonement to cleanse and heal me from what Daddy had done."

"So," Darren said, getting back to the steps, "first she had to recognize that what had happened was wrong. She had to clarify which things she was responsible for and which ones were not her fault. In her case, Liz was not to blame."

I broke in. "That was something Darren helped me clear up. When we got married, I was lost in confusion and honestly feared the abuse had somehow been my fault."

"Okay," Ben said, jotting something down in his black notebook. "You recognized it and clarified it."

"The next step in repentance is feeling remorse."

"That shouldn't have been hard."

"No—that had been going on for years," I answered.

Ben's pen was poised above the page, "Third?"

"Confess, or reveal," Darren answered.

"I prefer to call this step 'stopping the lie,' " I said. "Whether the perpetrator still sees you every day or whether he's dead and gone, you have to tell the problem to those who can help you. I don't mean you have to wear a scarlet letter on your chest for the whole world to see, but these troubles can't get better if they never come out into the light."

"Who did you tell?" Ben asked.

"Well, first I told Darren. That was just about the hardest thing I've ever done."

"Anyone else?"

"Mom and Maria, and eventually, my stake president. Having to tell anyone at all didn't seem fair at first, because it wasn't my fault. But I discovered that there is healing power in speaking the truth. My secret didn't seem so dark when the right people knew it. They loved me anyway and actually understood me better."

After a brief pause, Darren went on, "Then there's restitution."

"Restitution?" Ben asked. "How would you handle that?"

"By allowing the perpetrator to answer for what he's done," Darren said.

"Oh, I see," Ben made another note in his book. "By not protecting him."

Restitution hadn't applied so much for me because Daddy was dead before I began healing. But there was another factor that had been especially significant.

"One more thing," I told Ben. "When a person repents of a sin he has committed, he usually forsakes it as an early part of recognizing and feeling remorse."

"True," Ben answered.

"But forsaking was perhaps the most difficult aspect of healing for me."

Ben looked at me quizzically.

"Don't get me wrong! I was trying with everything I had to keep from perpetuating the crimes I'd endured. But the real test, the hard thing, was becoming willing to forsake the pain. For a long time I didn't want to let it go."

"You didn't want to stop hurting?" Ben asked.

"Of course I did! But the injustices of my childhood were all etched in vivid detail across my mind. They were so unfair—I couldn't just snap my fingers and forget them."

"As long as they stayed, so did the pain," Ben murmured, almost to himself.

"Right," I said. "They shaped my view of the world, and it was a dismal one. But Darren was working on me all the time, extending another vantage point I hardly dared believe in."

/ / / / /

"Darren, I've kept my mouth shut for almost a year, now. Every month out of respect for your religious upbringing, I stifle my feelings. But I can't do it any longer." Pointing an accusing finger at the tithing receipt he was holding, I added with determination, "I forbid you to fill out that slip!"

"You what?" He stared at me in shock.

"I just can't let you keep doing this," I answered. "Every month you throw away a desperately needed part of our income. And now, this month the ward is asking for even more as a temple donation." I could feel the rising indignation that had been building up within me for nearly a year. "It isn't right! We need every penny we can get our hands on." Then, indignation turning to rage, I added, "In case you haven't noticed, dear, we're poor!"

Darren looked at me for a moment. Then, with his usual calm, he stood and walked out of the room.

I was furious. "Don't you try to ignore me, Darren Kearney! That money's mine, too!" I yelled after him. "I have a say in what gets done with it, and you're not going to spend it without my consent."

I'd hardly had time to catch my breath before he walked back into the room, carrying his scriptures and his seminary binder.

"Oh, no, you don't!" I raged. "You're not preaching to me again. I won't hear it. The scriptures are just plain wrong. I don't believe for a second that the Lord wants us to go hungry!"

"You *will* listen, Liz," Darren answered with infuriating composure. "Because half the money is mine and because I, too, have a say in where it goes." Pulling a small photocopied page from his binder, Darren handed me the sheet to follow along as he recited:

> Not mine to keep—not mine to spend,
> Not mine to give, not mine to lend,
> 'Tis the Lord's part—'tis the Lord's part,
> A tenth of all I gain.
>
> 'Tis His to have, 'Tis His to use,
> As He, not I, may please to choose,
> . . . .
>
> He gives me all and asks this part,
> To test the bigness of my heart,
> . . . .
>
> His part shall be the first and best,
> Of all the ten with which I am blessed.
> 'Tis the Lord's part—'tis the Lord's part,
> A tenth of all I gain.[1]

I stared at Darren with cold, fuming eyes. If he thought for one instant that some silly poem was going to keep me from being sensible—

"You see, Liz," he said in his steady, decided voice, "the money isn't ours to keep. It's God's."

I didn't see, and he could tell just by looking at me.

"Besides," Darren added firmly, "Right here in Doctrine and Covenants 64:23, it says, 'for he that is tithed shall not be burned at his coming.' Think of tithing as fire insurance for the Second Coming, Liz."

My cold stare didn't melt.

"Well, I for one, do not wish to be burned. Are you willing to take that risk?" Darren glanced over at Scottie's infant seat and directly back at me.

I could see by his eyes that he wasn't going to change his mind. I was amazed at his forceful stubbornness, because he didn't often hang onto things with such tenacity. Obviously, he was not going to be budged. So there we stood, at an impasse. While I was busy glaring at him, and he was still looking gently but resolutely back at me, the phone rang.

"Kearneys'," I said, picking up the receiver. "Well, hello, Sister Johansen! Yes, we'll be in town this weekend."

I listened as our friend explained that her husband was hosting a party for representatives of various political groups that weekend. Would I be willing to help her take care of the preparations? She needed someone to launder and press her linens, help with the housecleaning, and assist her in the kitchen during dinner.

Excitedly, I told her I would do it. If Darren was going to continue giving our money away, I figured I'd definitely need to increase our income. But even at that, I never dreamed what a blessing this job would be. Sister Johansen paid me two hundred dollars and asked if I would help again with her daughter's wedding the following month.

Shortly before payday, Darren was sitting at the table planning for the next month and balancing the last month's receipts. "Liz!" he said, turning toward me with the grin of a cat who'd swallowed a canary. "Look at this!"

Before him on the table was a simple spread sheet that looked something like this:

paycheck		$400.00
Johansen party		200.00
Total income		600.00
tithing	-60.00	
fast offering	-20.00	
temple fund	-50.00	
New balance		470.00
rent	-250.00	
utilities	-90.00	
groceries, etc.	-150.00	
Final balance:	-$20.00	

"So what are you gloating about?" I demanded, exasperated by his delight. "Obviously, I'm not getting grocery money. It's going to be another month of peanut butter and jelly or macaroni and cheese."

"You don't understand!" Darren was exuberant. "Those are our receipt totals, but somehow we still have ten dollars!" He reached into his jeans pocket and pulled out a rumpled green bill. "See? This is exactly enough for gas! We're going to make it to payday just fine," he announced, planting a million-dollar kiss on me.

Darren continued to glow about the confirmation of his faith, but I couldn't figure it out. We ought to have been twenty dollars in the hole, and we still had ten dollars left over. I *knew* we'd started the month flat broke. No matter how I figured it, those numbers did not add up. He persisted in calling this fluke a blessing, but I was content with the results of the coincidence.

During the months that followed, our lives got a pretty hefty serving of coincidences just like the unexplainable receipts. I did not think of them as the blessings that follow those who pay tithing, but Darren took every possible opportunity to point them out that way to me. I didn't realize he was already plotting a path for our future—one that required a full tithe. Nor did I dream that he was praying that I'd see God's hand in our lives because he knew I needed to grow in faith if I were to travel that road with him.

I was so busy with everyday life and the sudden influx of jobs that followed my work with Sister Johansen (domestic help, weekend baby-sitting, house-sitting, etc.) that I never guessed what Darren was planning. The here and now required all of my energy.

Afraid of myself and the latent anger that smoldered within me, I was constantly reading books on parenting. I never hit my precious Scottie, but I often screamed with frustration. It seemed I couldn't deal with the past and cope with the challenges of the present.

Someone else was having similar troubles: Maria. We kept in touch by mail and then one day she called. "Liz, do you realize it's been more than a year, and Daddy is still the main topic of conversation around here?"

I wasn't surprised.

"Well, a lot of things have been coming out of the woodwork. From what I heard Grandma telling Mom, Grandpa seriously abused Daddy and all his brothers and sisters."

"Abused?" I asked. "Like how?"

"Physical, emotional, verbal, and so on. And the girls were sexually abused when they were little."

That didn't surprise me, either.

"Grandma Hughes told me it was her opinion that Daddy was seriously mentally ill, and with just cause."

"It's about time she caught on," I put in.

"But the rest of her opinion is that we need to overlook the things Daddy did to us and forgive him. It wasn't his fault."

My insides started boiling. "Maria! Do you realize what that means? Forgiving is forgetting. We'd have to forget everything! How are we supposed to do that?"

Maria didn't answer. But I was so angry I couldn't take this quietly.

"I still have nightmares, Maria! Did you know that? I wake up sweating and panting with terror. I still sleep in long, heavy pajamas no matter how hot it is. I have to watch every single move I make and double-think every thought so I won't do things the way he did."

The line hung silent.

"I don't want to become another link in the chain of victims-turned-abusers!" I fumed. "Don't you see? I could become like him unless I keep myself carefully under control. I feel like a diseased person who never knows when she'll start a plague. There's no way I can protect myself and my family if I just forget it all, Maria. Forgiving's forgetting," I said again. "I don't dare do that."

NOTE

1. George H. Brimhall, in LeGrand Richards, *A Marvelous Work and a Wonder* (Salt Lake City: Deseret Book Co., 1975), p. 394.

/ / / 26 / / /

suppose these steps for healing overlap quite a bit," Ben commented, writing in his binder.

"You bet," I answered.

"So, tell me where you began," Ben asked with a smile, almost teasing. "Did you two say, 'Let's start with the recognizing phase,' and then outline a plan?"

Darren leaned back in his chair, crossing his long legs and chuckling. "Hardly! Remember how I said we were led by the Holy Ghost? We followed each prompting, not knowing what would come next."

"And the first step?"

"Well, the first step and the ultimate goal were the only things that were clear to me. Liz wanted peace of mind more than anything else. We just had to find the road leading there. And the first step seemed to be helping her regain hope."

"Remember that term *soul-murdered?*" I asked.

Ben turned toward me, nodding.

"Well, that describes my life back then. I could no longer feel certain emotions—like joy. Anger and pain were familiar to me, but I dared not exercise joy. It seemed to have been crushed out of me over time. Perhaps it raced through my feelings sometimes—I'm quite sure I tasted it the first time I held Scottie—but I was powerless to recognize it, to hold onto it, or to create it."

"So what's that got to do with hope?" Ben pressed.

Darren smiled, took Ben's Book of Mormon, and leafed

through the pages. "Okay. In Moroni 10:22 it says, 'If ye have no hope ye must needs be in despair; and despair cometh because of iniquity.' " Returning the open book to Ben, Darren explained, "Liz needed to feel hope because hope leads to joy and faith. Hope is the opposite of despair, and despair grew out of the iniquity that had been forced upon her."

Although Ben was writing furiously, I was too excited to be patient while he caught up. "Hope is the beginning of resurrecting what seems entirely lost. Without hope we can't possibly exert enough faith in the Lord to have Him heal us."

Hearing my exuberance, Ben looked up, smiled at me, and then bent again over his notes.

"But we can begin with hope, applying the tools available to us and nurturing it. Then hope will give birth to trust and faith, and upon them Christ will add His grace, which is sufficient for everyone."[1]

/ / / / /

I wanted peace of mind so desperately that my desire consumed me, but for a long time, my spirit was too bruised to dare believe that this could be possible for me.

Half the time I wondered what planet Darren was from or if he would ever "get real." On the other hand, I wanted freedom from my chains badly enough that I was willing to do anything—even listen to what he was saying.

"Liz," he remarked one evening, "the ward's starting up a temple preparedness class. The bishop has invited us to attend, and I'd like you to go with me." His voice was as casual as if he were asking me to go to a movie with him.

But anything to do with temples reopened a powerfully sore wound in my heart. I glared at Darren with hate-filled eyes. "We've had this conversation before!" Slamming my book down on the end table, I growled, "I am *not* going to marry you in the temple and get myself locked into anything! I won't become some polygamist wife who has no opinions of her own and no self-worth! I don't have any intention of—"

"Liz," Darren interrupted, "I don't believe that what your mother said was true."

"How do you really know?" I retorted. "*You've* never been to the temple."

"No," he answered in his perturbingly calm voice, "I haven't. But I'm absolutely certain your mom misunderstood." He tried to put his arm around me—I shrugged him off. "Besides," Darren went on as if I'd kissed him instead of pulling away, "we can get all the answers to our questions from people who've been there. This class is the place to do it."

I shot him a long, stony stare as he walked over to the sink and ran himself a glass of water.

"Let's don't be afraid to hear both sides of the story," he added, after drinking it all.

"I'm not afraid!" I said. But I was.

I'd hoped for a celestial family once before. My prayers had been long and earnest, yet the wonder of the temple hadn't lasted and the love I'd felt there had fled. Maybe it was all nothing more than a little girl's dream. Maybe such things weren't really possible—at least not for me. The only thing I was sure of was I didn't want to open myself up to that pain ever again.

But Darren was insistent. Although I figured the best progress toward shaking off my chains would be found in self-help books, I went to Darren's class because he said answers were there, too. And after all, I *had* promised the Lord I'd do anything.

The teachers of the class frightened me. They said they knew this was true and that was true. They bore strong testimonies that intimidated me. But for some reason I kept going anyway, doubting and wondering. *Are they truly happy they've been to the temple?* I asked myself, trying to determine whether or not they, too, had second faces. *Why are they trying to get us to go?*

Behind everything the teachers said, I kept hearing my mother's voice: "Women are just possessions to kiss a man's feet. No brains and pregnant—that's what they want."

Then one evening, the lesson centered specifically on the importance of families being sealed. Our teacher's words were sharp, lancing cleanly to the core of my deepest pain. Being an eternal family in the celestial world was the ultimate reward, he said. That was the meaning of eternal life.

Tears began to course down my face as my heart burned. Two voices were struggling inside my head: my own reason and another voice—a whisper that I knew from so long ago.

I'm afraid, I said inside.

But this is true, the soundless inner voice answered warmly. *You don't have to be afraid of the truth.*

I don't want Darren to treat me badly! Maybe he will if I—

Darren loves you, my heart reassured me. *Things will get better.*

How can things get better? I wondered. *This is the best I've ever had. I don't want to lose it.*

Temple marriage is a deeper commitment to your relationship.

Right, I thought cynically. *I'll be stuck forever.*

No, the voice gently reassured. *You will be happy and together in the eternities.* These words burned with great force inside me. Suddenly I felt the same joy—that very wonderful, overwhelming joy I'd reveled in the day my parents and Maria and I had been sealed together.

No matter what fears gripped me, no matter what doubts filled my mind after the class was over, I couldn't deny how right that joy had felt.

/ / / / /

"Isn't it funny how we perceive ourselves?" I asked, changing the subject abruptly. "I mean, to make use of the tools available to us, we have to allow ourselves to leave our comfort zone. Of course I wanted to leave my comfort zone of fear and anger, to enter a trusting world filled with love and joy. But first I had to risk believing in myself enough to think I might be worthy of those hopes being realized. I was afraid to use the tools I had."

"Yeah," Darren said, laughing. "Can you believe this lady was worried about a long-term commitment with me?"

Ben grinned.

"If you'd said that back then, I'd have denied it," I admitted. "I was waiting and watching all the time for his second face to show itself. I just knew it was in there somewhere."

This time it was Ben's turn to change the subject. "Which tool were you most afraid of using?"

"Love," I answered without hesitation. "Yes, love. Allowing Darren to love me and nurturing the love I felt."

"How does love act as a tool?" Ben asked.

Does he have any idea how difficult his questions are? I thought to myself.

Darren saved me. "Research has shown that people cannot pull themselves out of compulsive behavior cycles alone.[2] They need a helping hand. And the Lord has said He will most often help us through another person."[3]

"Right," I broke in. "Every situation is unique. In my case, I had Darren to turn to. He was my source of the 'priesthood assistance' Elder Scott refers to."[4]

"What about those who don't have husbands who hold the priesthood?" Ben asked.

I didn't answer right away. Maria and Mom were in that position, and I had worried endlessly over their plight. "The Lord will provide caring priesthood leaders for every one of us, if we will seek them out," I said after some thought. "But don't forget, many women have family members who are willing to help. And talking things through with a therapist can also straighten out confusion."

"If they are chosen prayerfully, therapists can be important helpers for many abuse victims," Darren agreed. "They're trained to assist people in gaining a healthy perspective."

Ben asked, "Did you seek counseling, Liz?"

"No," I answered. "We could never afford professional treatment. But my sister Maria is in therapy right now, and I'm delighted. It's been so painful, watching my family struggle. I want to just walk into their lives and offer what I've found to make them feel better." I looked Ben right in the eye to make sure he understood how intensely I felt about this. "But I can't.

They're the only ones who can use the tools and let go of the pain. We each must do these things for ourselves."

/ / / / /

Despite my fear, I decided to take the chance. I agreed to be sealed to Darren.

Numberless obstacles hedged us in, threatening to prevent our trip to the temple. But we found ourselves humbled and grateful as friends and family rallied around us. In response to our prayers, an inspired solution answered each problem. Darren's boss reversed a policy that would have prevented Darren's getting time off. When our car died, transportation to Arizona was arranged. One of Darren's aunts even sewed a little white suit for Scottie and a lovely white dress for me.

Some of the hurdles were bigger than others. One particular incident nearly shook my confidence altogether.

We were at our first temple-recommend interview. Darren and I sat side by side, holding each other's hands, staring into the bishop's eyes, and waiting to hear the big question, "Are you worthy?"

Instead, he visited with both of us for a while before interviewing us separately. My interview was first, and then I waited outside the door during Darren's interview. I wasn't trying to eavesdrop, but when the bishop asked if there was anything in Darren's past or present that needed to be confessed and resolved, I was shocked to hear him say, "Yes." All my senses went on alert, and my hearing became astonishingly acute.

"What?" I gasped under my breath.

Darren's ever-calm voice was steady as he replied, "I've never confessed to a priesthood leader my part in Liz's being pregnant before we were married."

The bishop responded softly, and Darren must have turned his head or something, because I couldn't hear any more. I began pacing the hall furiously. Questions raced across my mind: *Is he sorry he's stuck with me? Is Scottie a daily reminder of his sin? Does Darren resent me for getting pregnant?*

I'd never regarded our premarital relationship as a bad thing.

After all, it wasn't as if I'd slept around. Darren hadn't been promiscuous, either. I'd told the bishop before we got married, but my confession hadn't been the unloading of a terrible burden—it hadn't been a confession at all, just plain fact.

As soon as we got home that evening, I let Darren have it. I felt his love for Scottie was in question, and that threatened me. I yelled at him and told him off, asking him every question I could think of. If he'd shown any sign of being ashamed of his beautiful boy, I'd have called everything off.

But Darren passed the test beautifully. My love and gratitude for him grew stronger. And another of the roadblocks between us and the temple was removed.

Caught up in what seemed a miraculous whirlwind, Darren and I finally found ourselves in Mesa at Eastertime. We went with his family to see the pageant on the beautiful temple grounds (we'd both seen it before), but our thoughts kept wandering from the performance to what was going on inside those sacred walls.

On the night before our session, I listened to the silence, wide awake in the guest room of Darren's parents' house. My husband rolled over and hugged me.

"Can't sleep, huh?"

"Sorry," I said, realizing how restless I'd been. "I didn't mean to keep you awake."

"Scared again?" Darren asked. I could just make out the hint of his smile in the darkness.

"Oh, Darren! It's not you, really! I love you. You've been wonderful to me—patient and kind. You have no idea what you mean to me."

"But you're still scared, and you can't forget what your mother said?"

How did he know? I was hearing her words in my mind right then, and the things she'd told me sounded like slavery. My understanding of the gospel was so innocent I didn't even realize that if Darren did indeed have a second face, I wouldn't be bound to him anyway. I'd not yet heard of the Holy Spirit of

Promise; all I knew was commitment when I was so afraid to trust.

"Darren," I breathed, and my words trembled in the still night. "I'm terrified!"

"I've been wanting to pray together in the morning, but maybe we'd better not wait until then. Would you join me, Liz?" he asked, sliding out of bed and onto his knees.

Darren stretched out his hand to me. "If you can describe your fears to Heavenly Father, He will send the Comforter to care for you tonight and tomorrow."

It always sounded so wonderful when Darren suggested we pray, but I was still uneasy with the process. After listening to Darren's eloquence, I felt like a toddler trying to explain my thoughts. I knelt beside him on the floor, but I couldn't bring myself to begin.

"Darren," I finally conceded, "I'm not sure what to say. I can't really describe how I'm feeling."

Even in the darkness, I could tell Darren was smiling again. "Liz, He knows. He just wants you to tell Him about it. Just talk. You don't have to be a poet."

Hesitantly, I began. As I made the first preliminary efforts to express myself, a calm feeling washed over me. Soon it became easy to explain myself, and I told Heavenly Father the things I believed happened in the temple. I held nothing back in describing my fear. And then I added, "Please help me understand the true meaning of the words that will be spoken. Please don't let me come out of Thy house feeling the way my mother did. I need to know I'm worth something to Thee. I want to come out knowing I did the right thing."

With surging emotion I concluded, "Please Father, I want an eternal family."

When the prayer was finished, we both knelt in silence. Then Darren put out his arms and pulled me close. As he did so, I brushed against his cheek and discovered that my face was not the only one bathed in tears.

NOTES

1. See Moroni 10:32.

2. For example, Martha Nibley Beck and John C. Beck have said of compulsive behavior cycles in their research: "We did not observe one case of a victim overcoming a compulsive cycle alone." *Breaking the Cycle of Compulsive Behavior* (Salt Lake City: Deseret Book Co., 1991), pp. 19–21.

3. "God does notice us, and he watches over us. But it is usually through another person that he meets our needs. Therefore, it is vital that we serve each other." Spencer W. Kimball, "The Abundant Life," *Ensign,* Oct. 1985, p. 3.

4. Richard G. Scott, "Healing the Tragic Scars of Abuse," *Ensign,* May 1992, p. 31.

/ / / 27 / / /

Thinking back on that tender moment of communion, I told Ben, "Prayer is a mighty tool—lots more powerful than we can guess until we've really invested in it."

"What strikes me as significant about prayer," Ben ventured, "is that it reveals our desire to trust God. The very act of praying showed you were making an effort toward hope."

"And it invited the Lord to intervene more directly in our lives," Darren agreed. "All these things reaffirmed our desire for help. Liz and I have noticed that whenever we make a point of watching for the answers to our prayers, and then give thanks for those answers, our hope and trust have grown."

/ / / / /

Early the next morning, I dressed Scottie in a cute romper and packed up his new white suit. As I washed his face, I noticed he was running a low fever.

"He's probably just teething," Darren's mother said cheerfully as we trundled all our things out to the car.

We drove through the temple gates, parked, and walked between the luscious-smelling orange and grapefruit groves toward the front of the temple. Suddenly, I found myself standing between the two crystalline reflection pools and the temple doors, with their striking ornamentation of gold circles.

It was all so marvelously beautiful that my breath caught in my throat. The same palm and date trees stood as majestic sentinels; the same clear sunshine danced across the temple walls and bas-relief carvings. My thoughts settled on those carvings of the pioneers pulling their heavy handcarts. Their struggles almost came to life in the play of morning sunlight, and—after all Darren and I had been through—I felt a sort of kinship to them, knowing we both understood heavy burdens.

The workers were as kind as they'd been when I was a child. We were meeting our escorts and shuffling recommends in the foyer, when Scottie suddenly squeaked and got sick right down the front of Darren's suit. Tossing me an uncomfortable grin, Darren announced, "It's not teeth."

"What do we do now, Darren? We can't send a sick child into the nursery! He'll be terrified! He's never had the flu, and he doesn't know any of these people—"

A tiny but capable-looking grandmother in white interrupted me. "Don't you worry, Mom. We'll care for this little darling as if he were our very own. We're equipped to handle any situation, you know."

I just stared at her. I hadn't known.

"It's going to take a whole lot more than a little flu bug to stop this day from happening," she said, scooping Scottie out of my arms with tender efficiency. "Go on now. You've come a long way for this."

You have no idea how far, I thought, as someone took my elbow. I had no family member who could attend the temple with me, so I'd asked Teri to be my escort. (She'd received her own endowment four months earlier, just before marrying a wonderful, returned missionary.) Linking her arm in mine, she smiled and led me toward the recommend desk. Our eyes brimmed with tears at being together again, especially in this place. After exchanging a long hug, we stepped into a waiting room and I looked around.

Darren's escort was his dad, and all his extended family was there—a very great number. My eyes were wet again, this time with awe at the support and love his family shared.

Perhaps it was my day for crying. I'm not sure if I ever stopped after that. The initiatory ordinances were a word-for-word answer to the prayer I'd asked the night before. The endowment made complete sense to me. I even understood the things my mother had misinterpreted and how she'd misunderstood them.

This day couldn't possibly be any better, I thought, admiring the huge bouquet of fresh-cut flowers in the soaring celestial room. Everything was so perfect.

"Darren," I whispered, as he kissed me, "this must be what heaven is like." My eyes traced the lovely, upward-sweeping lines of the walls, the sparkle of the lights. "I'm sure of it. Somehow Heavenly Father has given us a piece of heaven right here on earth."

Darren smiled. "Shall we go to the sealing room?" he asked. "Everyone tells me that's where we'll enjoy the most special ordinance of all."

There was standing room only at our sealing. So many family members and friends filled the room that I couldn't look up without crying. In a lovely, simple ceremony, Darren and I knelt across the sacred altar and were united for all eternity.

Then one of the workers from the nursery appeared at the door. "Your little Scottie got sick on the elevator just a moment ago. We'll have him cleaned up in a jiffy, if you'll just wait," she said.

Suddenly, I felt guilty. Had my baby been throwing up and crying all this time? I didn't have to wonder long. Soon the doors opened, and in came another sister, carrying Scottie. But instead of a sickly looking child, I was surprised to see him looking as bright and perky as ever. The Spirit swept over me once more, and I began to cry again. So did everyone else.

Following another ceremony, Darren and Scottie and I stood looking into the mirrors of eternity, as I had ten years earlier with my own mother and father. The Spirit whispered inside me just at that moment. More clearly than ever before, I heard these words: *This is the Lord's answer to your prayers, Liz. This is your forever family.*

/ / / / /

"Prayer gave me the courage to leave my past behind," I told Ben. "On the day Darren and I were sealed, the Holy Spirit showed me the answer to the prayers I'd offered for all those years—the ones I thought God had ignored."

"Prayers for a happy family?"

"Yes." I couldn't restrain my smile. "And along with this knowledge came some other, very important realizations. As we looked into the mirrors, I understood that 'God's delays are not God's denials.'[1] I also discovered I'd been harboring anger toward God. That was a shocking realization for me because I knew those feelings were unfair. God hadn't hurt me. Yet I had been so filled with anger that I didn't see until then that He had never abandoned me. As I looked back on my life, the Spirit showed me specific ways Heavenly Father blessed me, how the Comforter had been with me, how Christ had carried me through when my own strength was lost." No wonder I wept!

Ben nodded, sharing my happiness in that discovery. "Did it last?" he asked.

"Yes," I answered without hesitation. "I made a promise while we were standing beside the altar. I covenanted with God that I would keep myself temple-worthy. I also promised to be committed to my family. Being committed no longer meant being stuck—but it meant I wasn't leaving, either."

"I get the feeling your sealing in the temple was a very significant turning point in your life," Ben said.

"Oh, it was!" I answered. "After our trip to the temple, I started over from scratch. I felt I had to become truly converted to my religion. I could no longer be a Mormon if I went on thinking and doubting as I had in the past. The Spirit whispered to me that I needed to come unto Christ, so over the next several years I took advantage of every chance I could find to do that."

Ever analytical, Ben responded, "How?"

"Like with the scriptures," I answered. "I learned how to study them, not just read them. God doesn't put things on a silver platter and tell us to eat, you know. Adam was told he'd have to work for his supper, and that's true of spiritual bread, too. The answers to my questions were all there, but I had to study and pray and research to find them. Certain things come quicker than others. I'm still working on most of them."

Ben set his pen down on his open notebook and leaned back in his chair with an amused look on his face. "Liz, have you ever noticed that there aren't all that many scriptures dealing specifically with abuse?"

"Yes." I wondered what he was getting at.

"You just told me that *all* the answers are available if you use the tools," he added.

I could stand Ben's questions because he obviously knew the answers already. He just wanted to see what I'd say. So I echoed his grin. "I also pointed out that you have to work at it over time. The scriptures must be coupled with prayer. For example, I've heard it said that God never gave parents a handbook. But through prayer and study, I've found many scriptural instructions and insights into that very process."

"You win," Ben chuckled, leaning forward again and taking up his pen once more. "I can tell you *have* searched the scriptures and developed a testimony of prayer. I just wish I knew a way to dispense this kind of healing professionally."

"It might seem too obvious an answer, but the Lord really is the greatest physician of all," I said. "When you go to men, you get what men can do. And that's right, because we need to do everything in our power before we call on Him. But when you go to the Lord, you experience healing that only He can provide. Only He can ultimately heal us so perfectly that there won't even be scars."

/ / / / /

In time, Christ promises the faithful a perfect resurrection of both body and spirit. Until then, we need to work along the best we can.

Darren graduated with a degree in chemical engineering and a brand-new job right back home. I finished high school, graduating with a 3.7 grade-point average. Our family was blessed with three lovely daughters, another son, and many good years together. During all that time, I concentrated on recovering by coming unto Christ.

Heavenly Father blessed me with many opportunities for growth. While I was expecting our sixth child, I served in the Young Women organization. I loved working with the fine young women in our ward; I felt privileged to set personal goals right along with them. The values they studied seemed to be a tailor-made blessing for my own self-esteem, as well as theirs.

From the start, I discovered a soft spot in my heart for the girls who came to church alone. We had several part-member and less-active families, so I spent extra time getting to know the daughters in those homes. It hadn't been all that long since I'd been coming to church alone.

As I served those choice young women, I began to feel a deep love and concern for them. I could sense when a lesson touched off a spark of shame or hurt in their eyes. Because of my own experiences, my love did not change when I saw their troubles. Rather, I understood them. My gratitude grew with the discovery that I could be sensitive to hidden griefs that others might overlook.

"The value this month is integrity," our president said during leadership meeting. "We need to reinforce how important it is for a young woman not to jeopardize her integrity during dating experiences. So I've put together an object lesson to share in each class."

I watched as our president took a bunch of perfectly white rose buds and explained how they symbolized each girl and her own special beauty. White was, of course, to represent purity.

"Suppose the worst," she said, as if we were the class. "Imagine you slipped and lost your chastity and virtue." Dipping the rosebud into a bowl of black ink, she returned it to the bouquet of flowers. Its blotched petals sagged as a dark stain ran down the stem. "When a young man comes to choose his companion for eternity from this bouquet," she asked, "would this one be selected?"

I stared at her powerful presentation, tears flooding my eyes.

My purity had been stolen before I'd even reached dating age. There was a time when I would have identified myself as that tainted flower. What if one girl among our number suffered from those same scars?

Carefully, I explained to the sisters the dangers of this presentation. Talking to them from my own experiences, I asked, "Can we risk teaching this principle so callously?"

"Truth is truth," one sister said. "There *is* repentance."

"Yes, but we haven't illustrated that with our ink. When you need the Atonement's healing power through no fault of your own, black ink looks awfully harsh. Let's not dip the rose if we can't show its potential for being cleansed."

With care and a little more effort, we were able to alter our presentation to reach all the young women. To me, they really were like those tender rosebuds. I felt a great desire to protect them from pain caused by a lack of understanding or thoughtlessness.

But I also learned I had to protect myself the same way. Going to church required that I not let my feelings be hurt by the remarks of others. With time, I resolved that no one was going to take my testimony away from me. No matter how thoughtless someone else was, I could not afford to let others' words or actions stand in the way of my relationship with the Lord.

One night, while reading in the Bible, I found the story of John the Baptist sending two of his disciples to ask Jesus if He was "the one," meaning the Messiah, or if they should keep looking for someone else. Christ answered them with His miracles, pointing out that since He had come, the blind could see, the lepers were cleansed, the deaf could hear, the dead were raised, and the poor (who had previously been shut out of the synagogues) were being taught the gospel. Then He said something very curious, something that stuck in my heart and came to my mind many times afterward. He said, "Blessed is he, whosoever shall not be offended in me."[2]

I *had* been offended in the Lord. Until I was sealed in the temple, I'd blamed my pain on the One who wants my happiness more than anything. But my heart was comforted when I discovered that scripture. Someone may give offense, but I have determined that I will not take it. And I especially won't blame it on God.

When people say things now—usually unknowingly—that hurt me, I pray for them. I hope in time the Lord will gently teach them to understand.

/ / / / /

"Ben, do you know the story of Naaman?"

"The great servant of the king of Syria, who was also a leper? Yes, I know how he came to Elisha the prophet and was told to wash seven times in the Jordan river. Naaman wanted to know why the Jordan was different from any other river, but eventually he humbled himself and did it anyway."

"What happened when he washed?" I asked.

" 'His flesh came again like unto the flesh of a little child, and he was clean,' " Ben quoted.³

"Do you see?" I said, excited that he knew the story so well. "God has the power to heal wounds all the way! In His own time, the Savior heals spiritual wounds as completely as He healed Naaman. Not only was Naaman's skin as it had been before the leprosy, but his very flesh was as perfect as on the day of his birth."

"You're saying that blessings come with spiritual healing," Ben summarized.

"Yes," I answered emphatically. "As we go through that process, we discover we've progressed." Without giving Ben a chance to ask for specifics, I added, "I've still got scars. The process isn't over for me yet, but the wound is no longer a gaping hole. And along the way I've discovered that I have compassion and discernment I probably wouldn't have developed without knowing pain firsthand. I have a close relationship with the Savior and an appreciation of the Atonement that can come only from needing Him, getting to know Him, and experiencing His mercy. I wouldn't wish my experiences on anyone, but the Lord *can* use them to improve me. In fact, He promises He'll turn them to my good."⁴

NOTES

1. Years later, when I read this phrase in Robert Schuller's book, the Spirit filled me again. These words exactly expressed what the Spirit had taught me the day we were sealed. *Tough Times Never Last, but Tough People Do!* (New York: Bantam Books, 1983), p. 87.

2. Matthew 11:6.

3. 2 Kings 5:9–14.

4. "If the very jaws of hell shall gape open the mouth wide after thee, know thou, my son, that all these things shall give thee experience, and shall be for thy good" (D&C 122:7). "My grace is sufficient for all men that humble themselves before me; for if they humble themselves before me, and have faith in me, then will I make weak things become strong unto them" (Ether 12:27).

/ / / 28 / / /

I suddenly noticed Darren hadn't been adding anything to our conversation. Casting a glance in his direction, I saw he was still leaning back in his chair, but now his entire face was caught up in a grin. Even without words, his thoughts were clear to me. I knew my abuse had been the result of human decisions and moral agency—not something God had exploded on my childhood. But, here I was, talking to my doctor and husband about abuse as if it had been a prescribed treatment that had strengthened my spiritual self.

"Don't get me wrong, Ben. I really mean what I said about Heavenly Father's ability to take the most horrible affliction and turn it into a blessing. I know that for those who have faith, He will do that."

Ben glanced up from his notes for a moment, curious at the sudden change in my tone.

"This knowledge has been a great comfort to me after the fact. But getting to the point where I could even trust God or myself enough to believe these things is a whole different story. It has taken a long time—"

"Years," Darren broke in.

"And staying on top will be the work of a lifetime," Ben added. When Darren and I nodded, Ben thoughtfully tapped his pen a couple of times against his notebook. "I'm wondering what tools can help you stay on top of this. I mean, this abuse is like a horrible monster you've bashed into the ground. But throughout your life, aren't there times when it seems to rear its ugly head and haunt you?"

He understood so much! Then, before I could respond, he added, "And I bet you're going to tell me that using those same spiritual tools is the best means of handling this."

I nodded, wondering if there was some significance in the way we kept coming back to the same principles.

"So, I want you to name me three useful tools for keeping that monster's head down."

I glanced over at Darren and he smiled, apparently enjoying this. "Three of the most effective tools . . . ," I repeated, thinking. "Okay. Well, the first is obviously the one Elder Scott mentioned in his conference address—gratitude.[1] When I am troubled, I concentrate on all the good things I can find in my life—even the most miniscule, small things. The scriptures teach us that everything good comes from God, so I take that principle literally and give Him the credit. After I count my blessings, the Lord always seems to bless me with increased trust and faith, the things I need to keep going."

"I'll buy that," Ben said. "Second?"

"I still say the blessings of the priesthood are irreplaceable."

"For example?" Ben prodded.

"Um," I paused, my mind running back over the years. "Well, when I was fourteen, I received my patriarchal blessing. It might as well have been in French!"

Darren smiled. He remembered how I'd resented my blessing because it made no sense in my world.

"I didn't have any idea who Joseph was or why a tribe should be important to me. And the 'morning of the first resurrection' wasn't in my vocabulary. To be honest, I didn't understand a single word of it."

"So what happened?" Ben asked.

"Darren showed me how to look at it like a map. He taught me how to 'translate' it using prayer and scripture study and time as my compass. Eventually, I began to see that my blessing was an individualized guide containing information that could help me get where I wanted to be."

"Point number two, well taken," Ben smiled. "Three?"

Darren interrupted my mental search for the third tool. "May I name the third?"

"Sure!"

"During her childhood," he addressed Ben, "Liz fought against the bad things that happened to her."

At Darren's words my mind slid backwards. I remembered the day I'd quit pretending my chores weren't done when they were, the times Maria and I had run away, the terrible moments when I'd escaped prying fingers and dark eyes. I remembered how I'd hammered my five-year-old fist into the sky when the "silent treatment" succeeded. I felt the same elation now, except that victory wasn't mine alone. My triumph is built on humble, reverent gratitude.

Darren was still talking about what he thought should be the third tool: a determined attitude. "Liz wanted peace of mind more than anything. And she was willing to fight for happiness with the same vigor she'd summoned to survive the abuse. It took time for her to become Liz—not the formerly abused Liz."

"Sounds to me," Ben began, with his careful way of under-stating things he knew perfectly well, "like the healing process has, in many ways, been even harder than enduring the initial abuse. I mean, it requires more of the survivor because the person has to take the initiative. No longer are things just happen-ing to him or her. Instead, the survivor has to recognize what things he or she can control and make results happen there."

"You can't imagine how many times I've wanted to literally lie down and die," I said, the depth of my feelings clearly exposed in the sound of my voice. "But after I fought to keep going, I always discovered the Lord had been carrying me along. With hindsight I can honestly say that once I made the initial effort, He never let me down."

The room was silent again. Ben scrawled along the page for a moment and then was still.

"Ben? Can I share a story with you that I heard from a Finnish woman? It has everything to do with abuse—or rather, it has everything to do with moving on."

"You bet," he said, closing his notebook and folding his arms across his chest. "I'd love to hear it."

"Well," I began, remembering my wise friend's broken English, the kind music of her voice. "Once there were two men who met in the sunshine on the street. These men often spoke of important things. And one day one of them said, 'Good and evil are like two dogs inside me, clawing and biting and snarling.'

" 'Oh?' his companion asked. 'Which one wins the fight?'

The first man looked at his friend with candid eyes and answered simply, 'The one I feed.' "

/ / / / /

The summer of 1990 was a hot one in Boulder, Colorado. We'd moved there so Darren could take a position at Rocky Flats. He was spending a lot of time getting started at his new job, so he flew the twins up to help us. I was well into my sixth pregnancy and discovering the same frustrations my mother had felt when she'd had to stay down. Doing nothing was driving me crazy. And, knowing I hadn't the willpower to follow the doctor's orders, Darren had deputized Charlene and Vaughn for his personal police force.

They were fifteen years old now. Charlene was an easygoing young woman. For her, life was one day at a time, and she took everything in stride. But Vaughn was very sensitive; he seemed to carry his troubles on his shoulders.

With the differences in our ages and my leaving home when they were so small, I'd never developed a real bond with them as individuals. My relationship to them had been that of a big sister or a baby-sitter. So, even though this pregnancy was hard, I was grateful it had given me a chance to get to know them. And I still had no idea what a blessing they would be to me.

Late one summer evening when Charlene had gone off to play volleyball with some of the youth from our new ward, Vaughn helped me put the children to bed. After they'd all had a bath and a drink and said their prayers, Vaughn and I went outside to sit on the steps where it was cool. The only sound in the darkness was an occasional car or the whirr of a cricket.

"Liz," Vaughn asked, interrupting our companionable silence. "Can we talk?"

"Sure," I answered, a little surprised and concerned by the intensity of his voice.

It seemed to take a long time for Vaughn to continue, as if he had to work up to vocalizing what was on his mind. "I . . . I want to know what my dad was like, Liz," he said at last, looking up at me with searching eyes. "Every once in a while someone slips and makes a negative comment, but for the most part the subject seems off-limits. Why?"

Vaughn's earnest voice cut sharply through the dark August night. Guilt penetrated my heart as I realized for the first time that I'd never said a single good thing about his dad to him, or to his sister, either.

As I looked into Vaughn's face, a pale oval in the light of the streetlamp, his eyes revealed the depth of his need. He craved knowledge of who he was. He yearned to know that he had been loved.

Even as my heart went out to him, a shudder ran through me. Vaughn looked so much like his father: light brown, close-cropped hair, the intense, searching gray eyes, the latent physical strength in the movements of his young body. Even the ears—! But there was something different from what I remembered in my father—something humble and vulnerable.

"Vaughn," I began. Why was my mouth suddenly so dry? "Vaughn, I—"

My mind sailed back into the past, to a time I'd tried to bury. I did not want it intruding on my here and now. Not that I'd forgotten it, but, rather, I hadn't let myself dwell on those things after our wonderful day in the temple.

Now, as my thoughts rushed back over the years, I was looking for something I'd never seen before. I was hunting for goodness. The longer Vaughn's intent, longing gaze remained fixed on me, the more feverishly I tried to find something—anything that would encourage him.

"Well, Vaughn . . . " Inwardly I begged Heavenly Father for help. "It . . . it's not easy for me to . . . well, I, uh—" My stuttering slowly gave way to smooth, regular speech. "The greatest quality about your dad, Vaughn, was his knowledge. He was extremely intelligent—very! Even when something didn't come easily to him" (I was remembering all those high school and college tests), "he mastered the task at hand. Years after he'd taken a test, he could still pull his textbook off the shelf and turn straight to the page where specific information was."

Vaughn's face relaxed a little as I went on talking. His hands slowly moved from where they'd been clamped around his bent legs. Soon the elbows were braced against his knees, and his chin rested in his cupped palms.

"Your dad was a hard worker, you know." I went on, being careful not to say something just because I had a desire to please Vaughn. Whatever I said *had* to be true. And although the process was painfully difficult, I was discovering it wasn't impossible. The person I'd hated for so long, the man I'd once vowed never to forgive, did in fact have some good qualities. "He was very neat, too. He took meticulous care of himself and his things. He had a fantastic sense of humor. Did you know that?"

Vaughn shook his head and smiled. "Nah, really?"

"Really! People liked being around him. He made them laugh and relax. He knew how to have lots of fun." After I told him about the Wild West party and how he taught me to dance and some of the funny things Daddy had done while chaperoning our swing-choir tour, we were quiet again. Then I got around to the obvious. "You look a lot like him, you know." I grinned and rumpled his hair. "Spitting image."

"Yeah," Vaughn answered, not minding what I'd done to his hair. "Grandma told me that."

"Know what else?" I asked, and my voice wavered. Tears sprang into my eyes as this boy looked up at me with sweet innocence. "Your dad loved you. He really did. I'll never forget the day he blessed you two. He was so proud of you! Everyone could see that he loved you very, very much."

Vaughn's eyes were wet. Tears began to slide down his smooth cheeks.

I went on, my face soon as wet as his. "Your dad baptized me, you know. He baptized me and Maria and Mom. That was perhaps the most important thing anyone has ever done for me," I said, realizing that Mom had never taken the twins to church. "Besides Mom's giving me birth, the gospel is the most precious gift anyone ever gave me. That and my family—all the people I love so much. The day Daddy baptized me was very special. After that, nothing in my life was ever quite the same again."

We talked for a long, long time that night. Vaughn asked me questions about Chuck's likes and dislikes, about his work and his hobbies. There were a lot of words said, but the conversation meant much more than a dialogue about Daddy's interest in horses and inability to cook. Something happened inside for both Vaughn and me—something wonderful.

For weeks afterward, our conversation stayed in my mind. Although it brought peace to both of us at the moment, it left me somewhat uncomfortable, too. I tried to bury the memory of our discussion, but it kept hanging around the back of my mind. And every time I let myself think about it, I realized that the terrible monster I'd despised so long had actually been a human being. He was a father. He'd once been a tender child. There were admirable things about his character. In fact, there were things he'd taught me—things I'd emulated.

Like the man in my friend's story, I had two dogs inside me, and even as I had been seeking to return to the presence of God, I'd nurtured hate within myself. That irony was something I simply couldn't ignore. But I didn't know what to do about it, either. Forgetting all those injustices wouldn't be a fair solution. They were real, and they *had* hurt.

So I threw myself with increased vigor into my family and my Church callings. I tried to keep busy every second, even though I was presumably laid up. And through it all I prayed for understanding, for peace.

One beautiful afternoon the kids were playing down at the

park. In spite of doctor's orders, I couldn't stand to just lie around. So I went into the kitchen to wash dishes. Sunlight slanted through my window and made rainbows across the soap bubbles. It felt so good to sink my hands into the water, right up to the elbows.

I'd been asked to sing in church that Sunday, and so, as I enjoyed that simple, routine chore, I began practicing my song:

> Jesus was no ordinary man.
> But there were some who did not understand.
> They saw Him working miracles,
>   but some were still deceived.
> Why did they not believe?
>
> When with few loaves and fishes the multitudes were fed;
> When He showed them His pow'r to heal,
>   and even raised the dead;
> When He walked upon the water
>   and He calmed the raging sea,
> Why did they not believe?
>
> When His faith filled the fishnets;
>   gave sight unto the blind;
> When they saw at His bidding
>   even water turned to wine;
> When He offered all He had to them
>   if they would but receive,
> Why did they not believe?
>
> *Jesus was no ordinary man.*
> *The pow'r to bless and heal was in His hands.*
> They saw Him cleanse the leper;
> They saw Him heal the lame;
> They must have sensed divinity
>   and known from whence He came,
> But understanding not His cause,
> They crucified the Son of God,
> And even then they did not understand that
>   Jesus was no ordinary man.[2]

My hands were idle in the dishes; my tears fell among the

pretty bubbles. How many times I had sung that song before! And yet never, never had I felt the way I did right then.

I knew the story; I understood the events of the Savior's life. But at that instant something spoke to my heart and told me much more. I'd always known the accounts of His life were true, but until that moment I'd never really *felt* it. I'd tried to draw closer to Christ by understanding the events of his life. Now I knew I had to grow closer by coming to know *Him.*

And in that simple fact lay all the healing I'd been seeking for so long.

NOTES

1. Richard G. Scott, "Healing the Tragic Scars of Abuse," *Ensign,* May 1992, p. 32.

2. Janice Kapp Perry, "No Ordinary Man," *The Light Within,* 1985, pp. 15–17; emphasis added. Used by permission.

/ / / 29 / / /

T hose two dogs are inside each of us," I explained to Ben. "And being ambivalent toward them won't make us more like Christ. We can't feed both dogs and expect goodness to win. We can't have love and joy fill our lives if we're nurturing ha—"

Blip! Blip! Blip1

I jumped six inches at the loud beeping sound coming from Ben's belt. Smiling, he reached down and shut off the buzzer on his pager. "Excuse me," he said, walking behind his desk to reach the phone.

"We'd better scoot," Darren said, looking at his watch.

"Wow," I breathed, following his line of thought. I'd lost all track of time. Options for our date were now down to a very late movie or a dessert, but Darren didn't mind any more than I did. We slid our coats back on and moved toward the door.

"Looks like Jennie Finch has broken her leg," Ben said, after hanging up the receiver. "I need to meet her family down at the hospital."

"Oh," Darren said, "that's too bad." He swung the office door open for me, and we stepped out into the hall.

"Maybe it's just a fine fracture," Ben added, zipping the case of his planner shut. He pulled his coat on and began buttoning it, turning the collar up against the cold. He flipped off the lights and locked the office door with that ponderous set of keys.

"Listen," he swung around to face us once more, "it's been good talking with you—really good."

I looked again at Ben's face as he reached out to shake our hands. He seemed lighter, brighter now than when I'd discovered him standing in the hall. I remembered how one of my friends always says abuse is a disease that can be cured by talking about it, by bringing it out of the shadows, exposing it for what it is, and realizing what can be done about it.

"Maybe we'll talk about this again sometime," Ben added, as if he'd read my thoughts. "Can I call you if I ever write that book?"

"Absolutely!"

He pushed open the bar-handle of the foyer door, and a rush of bracing air swept in. "It sure is a blessing to know a pair of honest-to-goodness chainbreakers," he grinned, and we all stepped out into the swirling snow.

When had snow begun falling? I wondered vaguely. Chainbreakers. As I watched Ben disappear into the whirling white flakes, my mind tumbled back one last time to the day when the biggest chains had been cut from my life, the day I'd finally let them go.

That was during a flu season, too. In fact, the summertime bug got me down not long after Vaughn and I had talked. The virus hadn't upset my stomach much, but I did have an irritating, exhausting cold that seemed to drag on and on.

One afternoon contractions set in after a fit of coughing. Eventually, because they didn't let up and because I was bored, I began timing them. Although irregular, they kept coming, again and again.

Frustration welled up beneath my tiredness. No matter what I'd done during this pregnancy, it seemed as if my body was always threatening to go into labor. Now I couldn't even find a way to lie in bed without having contractions.

Finally I closed my eyes tightly against the pain and started praying. I explained to Heavenly Father that I felt I simply couldn't take this anymore. I told Him I was beyond the limits of exhaustion that my physical self could endure. The baby wasn't due yet, and I wasn't sure if I should take these contractions seriously. Was there something wrong? Could He tell me whether I needed to be worried or not?

When my prayer was finished, I rolled over and tried to breathe deeply.

"Hi there!" Darren said, coming around the corner.

"What are you doing home already?" I asked, surprised and wondering if this was the Lord's answer to my prayer.

"Oh, I don't know," Darren responded with smiling eyes. "Just thought you might like to see me." Looking around, he added, "Where are the kids?"

"At the pool with Vaughn and Charlie." Then another spasm clenched inside me. "Darren," I said, my breath catching in my throat. "Maybe you were inspired to come home. I'm having labor pains again."

"I can see," he answered, sitting down on the bed beside me and taking my hand.

When the pain passed I added, "I was just about to call the doctor. I think he'll want me to be checked again."

At five-thirty the next morning our new arrival cried out with such a big wail that everyone in the room was soon chattering about her lungs being well developed for a "preemie." And she weighed in right at six pounds—much bigger than the doctor had expected.

But I had a funny feeling about it all. My little darling kept gasping and making raspy noises. "Is she okay?" I asked the pediatric nurse.

"Oh, yes," she said, exuding confidence. "I think so." She thumped my baby on the back and cleaned out her mouth one more time, checking for phlegm. Then she said, "Say, how about if I take this angel straight to the nursery and have a doc check her out, just as a precaution?"

"Please," I said, wishing I could hold my new daughter at least a moment longer in spite of my suspicions.

But I had to stay in surgery after my baby was gone. I have a horrible record of overreacting to drugs, and this was no exception. When the anesthesia was administered, my whole body tried to go to sleep. The nurse yelled at me and squeezed my hands and arms. "Breathe, Liz! Breathe!" She put an oxygen mask over my face and shouted in my ear, "You have to stay awake, Liz!"

The oxygen and her yelling stopped me from slipping away, but I felt tired beyond explaining, almost beyond caring.

After a couple of hours they considered me stable enough to return to my room, still on oxygen. As they wheeled me in, unfamiliar faces began introducing themselves. Among them were a neonatologist, the hospital counselor, and the head nurse from the newborn intensive care unit. My new daughter, they explained, had the same virus I had. Her pneumonia was so advanced that one lung was full, the other half-full. Darren was down in intensive care with her.

A very strange feeling encompassed me as they each shook my hand, promising to come back and answer my questions when I was more rested. In the empty silence of the sterile room, my mind told me I ought to be worried. Yet my heart was whispering something far different.

Was I just too tired to cope? Was I slipping away from caring about things the same way I had in surgery?

But in my mind the song I'd sung only days before was running on and on. "Jesus was no ordinary man. . . . The power to bless and heal was in His hands . . . "

I reached for the bedside phone and called my former visiting teacher, who had become my best friend. "Hi, Judy, it's Liz." After the regular questions about sex and length and weight, I explained that our newborn was seriously ill. "Could you do me a favor, Judy? I need Phil to come down and help Darren. I think the baby needs a blessing."

Then I asked the nurse to call Darren in from the newborn intensive care unit. When Phil arrived, the two of them gave our new daughter a blessing.

"You have quite a miracle on your hands!" the neonatologist announced some time later, without suspecting just how accurate his choice of words was. "The antibiotics haven't even had time to kick in yet, but apparently they have. Your little girl is already coming out of the woods."

The head nurse was with him, and she smiled at me. Perhaps she recognized the origin of that miracle. "How long has it been?" she asked, looking at her watch. "Only about three hours?"

The doctor beamed. "Mm hm. Really amazing. One lung is clear; the other, halfway."

After they were gone, I lay for a long time, peaceful and warm. I knew where the miracle had come from. And the music was still playing over and over in my mind, "The power to bless and heal was in His hands . . . "

Like most spiritual experiences, this was a simple event. There was no lightning or thunder. No court of law could prove my baby's recovery had been the result of divine intervention. But the Spirit whispered unmistakably to my heart. Like the night Vaughn and I had sat on the steps, like the day I'd been singing while washing dishes, something significant was happening inside me.

Through this miracle, all the things I'd been studying about the Savior were suddenly very real and immediate. Something I'd read weeks before sank into my mind as if I were hearing the words for the first time: "In addition to bearing our sins . . . Jesus [came] to know our sicknesses, griefs, pains, and infirmities as well. . . . Jesus . . . not only satisfied the requirements of divine justice but also . . . demonstrated and perfected His capacity to succor His people and His empathy for them. He came to know, personally and perfectly, 'according to the flesh' how to help us become more like His fully comprehending Father."[1]

The price Christ paid in Gethsemane not only endowed Him with a perfect understanding of all our struggles but opened the way to salvation. His sacrifice and empathy bought us eternal possibilities. "We were literally purchased by Jesus," I whispered to myself, recalling the words of Elder Maxwell.[2] But for once I wasn't repeating what I'd heard others say. For once it was real.

I meant it. In my heart I knew it, and somehow through the Spirit, I understood it. "We were literally purchased by Him!"

Without realizing it in so many words, I now had the necessary faith and strength to take a big step in my own healing. Until then, I'd been using a file on my chains, but in that moment it was as if the Savior had handed me a cutting torch. With it, I could reach out and sever those heavy bands.

/   /   /   /   /

After only four days, my newborn daughter and I were discharged from the hospital. What my doctor insisted on calling an amazing coincidence, I knew to be a miracle. A few weeks later, when life was again functioning in a semiorganized fashion, Darren stayed home with the older children, while the baby and I drove the twins home to Arizona. After visiting my mother and letting her see her newest granddaughter, I planned to return straight to Boulder. But before I left Mesa, I made a little detour. The distance wasn't far, though I followed a route I hadn't taken in nearly fifteen long years.

Every detail of that day stands out vividly in my memory. The sun was shining bright and hot, the trees and lawns were deep green, and the flowers around people's houses seemed to radiate vibrant color.

I turned in between a set of white gates and drove slowly along the narrow, palm-lined path. This was a very reverent place. Baby Betsy seemed to sense it, too. Even before I pulled over to the side of the road, she was sleeping peacefully, sucking her lower lip. I opened the windows and turned off the motor. Carefully, I eased out of my car and walked a few yards across the lawn. I read the names on the stones as I went, until I reached my father's last resting place.

I stood above the marker for some time, quiet with my thoughts. I clearly remembered the last time I'd visited this place. It had been such a dreary day: cool, misty, angry. Today's warm peacefulness made an almost overwhelming contrast. I sat down on the soft grass beside his grave.

"Well, Daddy," I said, not realizing at first that I was talking out loud. "Here we are, and it's been a long time. I don't think a day has passed since you died that I haven't thought of you. I wish I could say they'd been good thoughts. It's only been recently that I've even *tried* to have any good thoughts."

A pretty little bird with red on its wings flew down and landed on the headstone. It hopped up and down for a moment, chirped, and then flew off.

"I don't feel as if I ever really knew you," I went on. "There were so many secrets. I'm sorry your childhood wasn't a good one. I'm sorry your life in general wasn't very happy."

I hadn't planned what I was going to say, but I wasn't searching for words, either. I had something to tell him, and it felt as if Daddy was listening.

"The things you did to us hurt us a lot. Even after you died, they caused us so much pain! For a long time, that pain and anger were destroying me. But then I began to realize I can't allow that to happen. I don't really understand all your anger; I don't know all the pain you've endured. But I do know there's Someone who does. You can draw near Him where you are."

The little bird swooped past again, gliding low and then up into the palm trees that lined the road.

"I'm letting you go, Daddy," I explained, and my voice cracked. Tears of peace began streaming down my cheeks. "God can take care of the past," I said, and for the first time I truly meant it. "The past is behind me now. Maybe you were suffering and ill. Maybe you were bound by chains and unable to free yourself. If so, I know we'll meet in the eternities. But if you were wrong and responsible—" my voice cracked again and I sat crying for a moment, compassion washing over me, cleansing me on the inside. "Please, please, Daddy, make the changes you need to and seek to be forgiven."

After letting the silence lie for a while, warm around me like the sunshine, I went on. "I forgive you for the past, Daddy. All the wrongs and all the pain and all the sadness are burdens I'm not going to carry any longer. I'm turning it all over to the only truly just Judge. It's between the two of you now."

Standing, I smoothed my skirt. I could hear the little bird

singing overhead somewhere in the palms. "Good-bye, Daddy," I said.

As I turned to walk away, tears still flooded my cheeks. But they were so different from the hard, angry feelings I'd had the last time I'd visited this place. The walk to my car was easier than before. The chains that had bound me were cut loose. I felt light and free, much as I'd felt the day I'd risen from the waters of baptism. Life was going to be great.

I was alive again.

NOTES

1. Neal A. Maxwell, *Not My Will, but Thine* (Salt Lake City: Bookcraft, 1988), p. 51.

2. Neal A. Maxwell, *All These Things Shall Give Thee Experience* (Salt Lake City: Deseret Book Co., 1979), p. 28.